Presented To:

Dad

From:

Father's Day June 18, 2000

Date:

Happy Father's Day!
We love you so much!
Love,

Janet, Brian
Tim, Kevin, Mary

# God's Little Devotional Book on SUCCESS

HONOR BOOKS
Tulsa, Oklahoma

*God's Little Devotional Book on Success*
ISBN 1-56292-267-X

P. O. Box 55388
Tulsa, Oklahoma 74155

Manuscript compiled by W. B. Freeman Concepts, Inc., Tulsa, Oklahoma.

Printed in the United States of America.

# INTRODUCTION

This book is about success, the reason to read it, however, is *motivation.*

A person's success is deeply rooted in their individual gifts, traits, and desires. It is related to each person recognizing their unique potential and working to fulfill it, while holding to the values associated with it, and accomplishing goals on the path toward it. Therefore, each person's definition of success is different.

There are many methods for becoming successful, but they all contain these four basic truths in one form or another:

- be your best (noble character),
- do your best (quality performance),
- work hard (quantity of performance), and
- never give up (persistence).

The definition of success and methods of attaining it are individual, but common to every person's pursuit of success is the need for *motivation.*

One must have constant motivation to do what is right, to seek to develop the most noble character possible, especially when our culture as a whole seems to be in moral decline. One must have a continual motivation to do one's best, when slipshod work easily passes in many circles, workloads are heavy, and deadlines are pressing. One must have consistent motivation to work hard, when "taking it easy" is always a temptation. One must have a ceaseless motivation to persist and endure, when giving up promises less stress and more fun.

If we are going to reach our potential, we must overcome our own inertia, our own "status quo."

The apostle Paul knew this. He advised Timothy, his son in the Lord and companion in the ministry, to "stir up the gift of God which is in you" (2 Timothy 1:6 NKJV). The quotes, scriptures, and devotions in this book are aimed toward that end — to "stir up" your gifts, talents, and godly ambition, so that you might become all your Creator designed you to be.

No one can make you into the person you desire to be, dream of becoming, or are destined to be, except you, and to the extent that you allow Him to do His work in you, the Lord Jesus Christ. Be encouraged. You *can* be more, do more, and achieve more. Stay *motivated!*

Blessed (happy, fortunate, prosperous, and enviable) is the man who walks and lives not in the counsel of the ungodly [following their advice, their plans and purposes]...

■■■

*But his delight and desire are in the law of the Lord, and on His law (the precepts, the instructions, the teachings of God) he habitually meditates (ponders and studies) by day and by night...and everything he does shall prosper [and come to maturity].*

Psalm 1:1-3 AMP

Psalm 1 presents two approaches to life. One is scornful, negative, pessimistic, and cynical. The psalmist says the person who walks this way has shallow roots and withers when a dry season comes, because he has no true source of nourishment for his life. The other way is happy and accepting of the things of God — principled, grounded in truth, and filled with delight in the Lord. The person who follows this way is likened to a tree planted near a steadily flowing stream. His roots are always supplied with life-giving water and, therefore, they grow deep. The blessed person lasts in times of trouble or drought and prospers.

In the psalmist's second analogy, the person who leaves God out of his life is like chaff blown away by the wind. Nothing he does lasts. He has no staying power. Nothing truly satisfies him or seems worthwhile. He moves from fad to fad. The implication is that those who embrace God and the things of God are like good grain that produces, multiplies, and creates something of lasting value for himself and others.

The Bible definition of success does not lie in what a person accomplishes, but the nature of the *relationship* that a person has with God, which in turn provides the *reason* for the effort a person expends. Evaluate your life today. Where are you planted?

# Success in the world means power, influence, money, prestige. But in the Christian world, it means pleasing God.

■■■

*And whatever we ask we receive from Him, because we keep His commandments and do those things that are pleasing in His sight.*

1 John 3:22 NKJV

John Houston has written his friend Myrtle's name next to Psalm 30 in his Bible. This psalm declares, in part, "O Lord my God, I called to you for help and you healed me. O Lord, you brought me up from the grave; you spared me from going down into the pit." After a hard-fought battle against cancer, Myrtle died shortly after she had underlined these words in her own Bible.

Myrtle was not a "success story" of miraculous healing. Nevertheless, in Houston's opinion she experienced true success. He writes, "At her funeral service, instead of banks of flowers there were groups of people who had witnessed her love of God. One group was there because they had all discovered faith in Jesus through the way she lived. Another group was thankful for her teaching in a Bible class. Another group remembered how she had shown hospitality. Still others were there because they had seen her transcendent spirit as she fought her long, painful illness."[1]

The true success story in each of our lives is our coming into relationship with God, who intervenes in our lives, helping us to overcome with His Word, the Bible, changing our attitudes and transforming us into people with whom He desires to live forever. In His presence, we find help, healing, and deliverance that last *forever.*

# Success isn't measured by the position you reach in life; it's measured by the obstacles you overcome.

■■■

*Blessed is the man who perseveres under trial, because when he has stood the test, he will receive the crown of life that God has promised to those who love him.*

James 1:12

In 1927, Lucille Ball was told by an instructor at the John Murray Anderson Drama School, "Try any other profession. Any other."

Academy Award-winning filmmaker Woody Allen flunked motion picture production at New York University, *and* at the City College of New York.

Universal Pictures dismissed both Clint Eastwood and Burt Reynolds in 1959, claiming that Reynolds had no talent and Eastwood talked too slow.

Malcolm Forbes, the late editor-in-chief of *Forbes* magazine, failed to make the staff of his school newspaper when he was an undergraduate at Princeton University.

Decca Recording Company executives responded negatively to the audition of four young musicians, saying, "We don't like their sound. Groups of guitars are on the way out." The Beatles took their sound elsewhere.

For seven years, a young inventor named Chester Carlson took his idea to twenty corporations, all of whom turned him down. The Haloid Company finally purchased the rights to his electrostatic paper-copying process. Haloid became Xerox.

Don't be discouraged if you are not finding the acceptance and success you desire today. Your success story is still being written!

# Effort is the supreme joy. Success is not a goal, but a means to aim still higher.

■■■

*I know that I have not yet reached that goal, but there is one thing I always do...I keep trying to reach the goal and get the prize for which God called me through Christ to the life above.*

Philippians 3:13,14 NCV

When Gene Stallings was the defensive backfield coach of the Dallas Cowboys, he had the opportunity to hear two All-Pro players, Charlie Waters and Cliff Harris, talking after a game against the Washington Redskins. Both men were sitting in front of their lockers after the game, which had been a very tough, fiercely-fought contest which ended in a close score. They were still in their uniforms, slouched over in exhaustion — too "spent" to even shower and leave the stadium.

Waters said to Harris, "By the way Cliff, what was the final score?" These men had played so intently, giving their all to the challenge before them, they hadn't stopped notice the points on the board.[2]

We all have heard the adage, "It matters not whether you win or lose, but how you play the game." Another twist on that saying might be: "*Everyone* who plays the game well, wins."

We *are* successful when we are faithful in giving our all to the values and goals we hold important. Success lies first in choosing a game worth playing, and then giving our best effort to that game.

# Success is 10 percent inspiration and 90 percent perspiration.

■■■

*The plans of the diligent*
*lead to profit*
*as surely as haste*
*leads to poverty.*

Proverbs 21:5

After five years as a sales manager, Bob was proud to say he had reached every quarterly income goal he had set. His territory had grown to include the entire state in which he lived. He had gained an excellent reputation among both his peers and competitors. Then, to Bob's surprise, his company reassigned him to a neighboring state.

The sales manager for that state had not worked very hard and the territory wasn't well developed. When Bob first heard the news, he saw it as a demotion. He wasn't at all *inspired* about this new task. His first impulse was to quit, but that passed quickly. Bob had always been a person who valued hard work — *perspiration* — so he rolled up his sleeves and got to work.

Bob put in long hours and lots of miles in the next few months, but by the end of the third quarter, his sales had surpassed those of previous territory. He had turned a trial into a triumph. Along the way, he developed associates who could help him maintain his success. The company rewarded Bob by naming him regional vice-president over both states, a position that would have been impossible for him to attain by staying in just one state![3]

Put your shoulder to the wheel. You never know where that wheel may take you.

# We can do anything we want to do if we stick to it long enough.

■ ■ ■

*You need endurance, so that when you have done the will of God, you may receive what was promised.*

Hebrews 10:36 NRSV

Phyllis Diller has written, "I was flying along great guns on my own, booking myself into those wonderful discovery clubs . . . then along came the 'Big Important Agency' with the big guns and they booked me into places where I shouldn't have been, for a lot more money, but for total failure. One such place was the Fontainebleau Hotel in Miami Beach, at its peak when they were playing top entertainment — Frank Sinatra and his ilk. They booked me there and after my first show the manager fired me....

"My defeat positively paralyzed my big important agency. They thought...*We've picked a loser*. However, my being fired, so shattering at the time, turned out to be a really important break because 'The Tonight Show's' Jack Paar had just discovered me and liked me a lot. He believed in me. 'Out of work,' in New York, and available for that great NBC show whenever Jack wanted me — this was the absolute basis of my rapid rise to fame. Jack used me on the show so often, and each show we did was such a hit, they all later became reruns and the exposure was tremendous."[4]

Always think of a setback as one small step back that just might lead to two big steps forward!

# A diamond is a piece of coal that stuck to its job.

■■■

*When he has tested me,*
*I shall come out like gold.*
*My foot has held fast to his steps.*

Job 23:10,11 NRSV

When things go wrong, as they sometimes will,
When the road you're trudging seems all uphill,
When the funds are low and the debts are high
And you want to smile, but you have to sigh,
When care is pressing you down a bit,
Rest! if you must — but never quit.
Life is queer, with its twists and turns,
As every one of us sometimes learns,
And many a failure turns about
When he might have won if he'd stuck it out;
Stick to your task, though the pace seems slow —
You may succeed with one more blow.
Success is failure turned inside out —
The silver tint of the clouds of doubt —
And you never can tell how close you are,
It may be near when it seems afar;
So stick to the fight when you're hardest hit —
It's when things seem worst that
YOU MUSTN'T QUIT.[5]

—Unknown

If you quit today, you'll never know what lies just around the bend.

Failure isn't so bad if it doesn't attack the heart. Success is all right if it doesn't go to the head.

■■■

*A man's pride will bring him low, but the humble in spirit will retain honor.*

Proverbs 29:23 NKJV

A number of years ago, an aspiring writer interviewed Thomas J. Watson, the president of IBM. Watson gave him this advice: "It's not exactly my line," he said, "but would you like me to give you a formula for writing success? It's quite simple, really. Double your rate of failure.

"You're making a common mistake. You're thinking of failure as the enemy of success. But it isn't at all. Failure is a teacher — a harsh one perhaps, but the best. You say you have a desk full of rejected manuscripts? That's great! Every one of those manuscripts was rejected for a reason. Have you pulled them to pieces looking for that reason? You can be discouraged by failure — or you can learn from it. So go ahead and make mistakes. Make all you can. Because, remember that's where you'll find success. On the far side of failure."

Don't allow your failures or setbacks to discourage you. Failure need not be fatal. Arthur Gordon, the aspiring writer to whom Watson gave the advice, went on to become a well-known author and editor. He later said of Watson's advice, "Somewhere inside me a basic attitude had shifted. A project turned down, a lot of rejected manuscripts — why, these were nothing to be ashamed of. They were rungs in a ladder — that was all."[6]

# He who would climb the ladder must begin at the bottom.

■■■

*Anyone wanting to be a leader among you must be your servant. And if you want to be right at the top, you must serve like a slave.*

Matthew 20:26,27 TLB

In 1977, twelve-year-old Michael sat on a beach along the Gulf of Mexico and painstakingly put together a trotline — a maze of ropes to which several fish hooks can be attached. Meanwhile, his parents and two brothers were busy fishing. "You're wasting your time," they advised him. "Grab a pole and join in the fun."

Undaunted, Michael kept working at his tedious task, even though his family considered it of no value. At dinnertime, when everyone else was ready to call it a day, Michael cast his trotline far into the water, anchoring it to a stick that he had plunged deep into the sand. During dinner, his family teased him about coming away from the day's fishing empty-handed. But after dinner, when Michael reeled in his trotline, there were more fish than they had caught all together.

Seventeen years later, his patient persistence had taken Michael Dell from teen to tycoon. He became the fourth-largest manufacturer of personal computers in America, and the youngest man ever to head a Fortune 500 corporation. He got his start in high school when he bought his first computer and took it apart to figure out how it worked.[7]

Don't be afraid to start small. It's where you're headed that counts.

Step by step,
little by little,
bit by bit — that is the
way to wealth, that is
the way to wisdom,
that is the way to glory.

■■■

*Precept upon precept,*
*rule upon rule...*
*here a little, there a little...*
*the Lord will teach.*

Isaiah 28:10,11 AMP

The story is told of a small business owner from the old country who kept his accounts payable ledger in a cigar box, his accounts receivable on a spindle, and his cash in a simple cash register.

His son — trained in modern accounting methods and computerized spread sheets — said to him, "I don't see how you can run your business this way. How do you know what your profits are at any given time?"

The father replied, "Son, when I got off the boat, I had only the pants I was wearing. Today your sister is an art teacher, your brother is a doctor, and you're an accountant. I have a car, a home, and a good business. Everything is paid for. So you add it all up, subtract the pants, and there's your profit."[8]

There are very few (if any) "overnight successes." As one person has said, "There are only night after night after night after night successes...and on most of those nights, you'd better be burning the midnight oil."

Sustained and honest effort not only creates a foundation on which success can be built, but also an inner strength of character that enables you to handle success when it arrives.

# How can they say my life is not a success? Have I not for more than sixty years got enough to eat and escaped being eaten?

■■■

*For we brought nothing into this world, and it is certain we can carry nothing out. And having food and raiment let us be therewith content.*

1 Timothy 6:7,8 KJV

When Hyrum Smith was a boy, he lived in Hawaii. With its beautiful beaches, endless ocean, and warm breezes it seemed like Paradise. To an eleven-year-old boy, the sky was the limit; he felt he could do whatever he could imagine.

One day Hyrum decided to swim the 1-1/4-mile-wide Hanauma Bay. Feeling invincible, he set out through the 80-foot-deep waters. Then, the waves started swelling and he couldn't see where he was heading. About halfway across, he realized he had no energy left. He felt himself starting to drown.

Then, he saw a fin a few feet away. It was a shark! It's amazing how a person can find strength he didn't know he had when faced with the prospect of being eaten. Hyrum made it safely to shore because he realized, "It was okay to drown. It was *not* okay to get eaten." At that moment, success to him was not the triumph of crossing the bay. It was avoiding the shark.[9]

Take stock of your life today. The basics — sufficient food, adequate clothing, a roof over our heads — these are not blessings to take lightly. They should be considered a part of our success.

# The dictionary is the only place that success comes before work. Hard work is the price we must pay for success.

■■■

*Lazy hands make a man poor,*
*but diligent hands bring wealth.*

Proverbs 10:4

Most of his life, Thomas Edison worked 18-hour days. Until he was 65, he only took catnaps and occasional breaks to eat on most workdays. By the age of 75 he had cut his workday down to 16 hours, worked in two eight-hour shifts. He rarely slept for more than three or four hours a day, usually right in his lab. He sometimes lived in the lab for several days at a time. He once locked himself in a "lab prison" for 60 hours without food or water until he and his employees fixed a difficult problem. Work was the elixir of his life.

Pablo Picasso also produced vast amounts of work each day for most of his life. He painted 18 hours a day virtually every day until he was in his eighties. When asked why, he said, "I never get tired." At age 90 he was still producing works of art and told a reporter, "I don't have a single second to spare."

Albert Einstein felt there was never enough time for work. He was sometimes called an absent-minded professor, not because he was actually absent-minded, but because he relegated social and other events to the category of useless wastes of his time and energy. He regarded wearing socks as an unnecessary complication of life.[10]

All of these men, each great in his own field, envisioned success as nothing other than a by-product of their passion for their specialty and tireless effort.

# Have a purpose in life, and having it, throw into your work such strength of mind and muscle as God has given you.

■■■

*Live purposefully and worthily and accurately, not as the unwise and witless, but as wise (sensible, intelligent) people, making the very most of the time [buying up each opportunity].*

Ephesians 5:15,16 AMP

Idawalley Zoradia Lewis was the eldest of four children of Captain Hosea Lewis, the first keeper of the light in Narragansett Bay. In 1853, when Ida was fifteen, her father suffered a stroke, so she took over his job. Her main duty was to maintain the lighthouse's red beacon, which guided the great yachts of her era. She was also responsible for rowing her three younger siblings to and from school each day, a distance of some three hundred yards, regardless of weather.

The daily rowing proved to be good practice for the many rescues Ida made. Her first was to row out and scoop up four Newport boys, sons of wealthy families, who capsized their small sailboat. In 1866, she fished out a drunken soldier whose skiff had overturned. The next year, she saved three Irish sheepherders who capsized while trying to rescue sheep that had escaped from the herd along the shore. She also rescued the sheep!

Ida kept the lighthouse for fifty-four years and made eighteen rescues in all. The last one was in 1906, at age sixty-four. When asked once why she was willing to risk her life so often she said, "If there were some people out there who needed my help, I would go to them even if I knew I couldn't get back. Wouldn't you?" She kept the lighthouse for fifty-four years.[11]

Do you have a purpose that compels you to give *your* all?

# When success turns a man's head, he faces failure.

■■■

*Talk no more so very proudly, let not arrogance come from your mouth; for the Lord is a God of knowledge, and by him actions are weighed.*

1 Samuel 2:3 NRSV

When Kate was in elementary school, she was always at the top of her class. In high school, she earned straight A's and was valedictorian of her class. If anyone had asked her classmates, "Who's the smartest girl in your class?" everyone would have said, "Kate." The entire town expected Kate to earn scholarships and go on to college, so nobody was surprised when she did. They talked of her being Phi Beta Kappa and graduating summa cum laude some day.

At the end of the first semester, however, Kate's grades were one A, two B's, and two C's. She had never received a B or C before and she was so embarrassed she even considered dropping out of school. It took her three days to work up the courage to call her parents to tell them her grades.

After the initial shock wore off and her family convinced her to press on, Kate went to see a school counselor. She admitted that the competition was much stiffer at college than in her rural high school. She also admitted that her study habits were not the best. She worked hard, and by the end of her junior year, received all A's in her classes. She said of her accomplishment, "Since I didn't have to study much in high school I proudly assumed I'd never have to study much. I know better now and am glad for the lesson."

As you pursue success, don't let pride trip you up.

# The first step on the way to victory is to recognize the enemy.

■■■

*Discipline yourselves, keep alert. Like a roaring lion your adversary the devil prowls around, looking for someone to devour. Resist him, steadfast in your faith.*

1 Peter 5:8,9 NRSV

In 1993, a deranged fan stabbed tennis star Monica Seles, narrowly missing her spinal cord. She recognized her assailant as a man she had seen loitering around her hotel but she had no idea why he had attacked her. At the hospital, she couldn't stop asking, *What if he comes back?* That night, her parents and brother all stayed in her hospital room with her. Monica was assured that her attacker was in custody. Even so, she had flashbacks of his face, the blood-stained knife, and her own screams.

Monica did her best to stick to her physical therapy regimen, but she found it difficult to concentrate. She broke into tears at odd moments, and nightmares haunted her. Six months after the attack, her assailant was given two years probation and set free. Her fear intensified, and she sought out a psychologist to help her. Encouraged by her peers, she made a decision to return to tennis. Then came yet another blow. A German judge upheld her assailant's suspended sentence, which had been appealed. She said to herself, "Monica, you have to move on." It was time for a showdown with her fear. Three months later, she played an exhibition match, and scored two wins — one on the court, and one in her mind and heart.[12]

Are you facing an obstacle that seems insurmountable? Perhaps it's time to identify its source and face it head on.

# Everybody finds out, sooner or later, that all success worth having is founded on Christian rules of conduct.

■■■

*Glory and honor and peace*
*to every man who does good.*

Romans 2:10 NASB

A man once recognized Norman Vincent Peale on an airplane and told him that he had read his books and benefited from them. He then told Peale that he was a training supervisor and had spent a great deal of time listening to the problems of employees. He said, "I worked out six practical points for handling a problem. Would you like to know what they are?" Peale replied, "I sure would!" These are the six points he shared, which Peale in turn shared with millions of his readers:

1. When faced with a problem, pray about it, asking that God's will, rather than your own, be done.

2. Having prayed, believe that God will bring the matter out right.

3. Write the problem out in detail. This gives you a clearer view of it and prevents confusion.

4. Always ask yourself what is the right thing to do. Nothing that is wrong, ever works out right. Ask yourself if you are being fair to everyone concerned.

5. Keep thinking and keep working at the problem. First try one thing, then another, until you find a solution.

6. When your problem is solved, thank God. Give one-tenth of your income to God's work. When you give, God's blessings will be released to flow into your life.[13]

God has an answer for every problem you may face today, or will face in the future. He is ready to give you the solution and He is waiting to fill your life with blessings. Take it to God. He has an answer!

# By success, of course, I do not mean that you may become rich, famous, or powerful. I mean the development of mature and constructive personality.

■■■

*Perseverance must finish its work so that you may be mature and complete, not lacking anything.*

James 1:4

David Livingstone spent nearly all of his working life in Africa. He discovered Victoria Falls and Lake Nyasa, and wrote two best-sellers about his expeditions. Fame was never his dream, however. Far more important to him was the setting and reaching of his goals to explore the continent and see the abolition of the slave trade — and to do both without compromising his character.

Newspaper correspondent Henry M. Stanley met Livingstone less than two years before Livingstone died. He wrote of the time he spent with him,

> "His gentleness never forsakes him. His hopefulness never deserts him...His is the Spartan heroism...never to relinquish his work, though his heart yearns for home; never to surrender his obligations until he can write Finis to his work."

Stanley saw Livingstone's religion as "a constant, earnest, sincere practice...neither demonstrative nor loud" and one that was "always at work. Religion has made him the most companionable of men."

Thirty years of work in Africa kept Livingstone on his knees — in prayer. He counted his own character a matter of daily work, and considered it part of his daily success.[14]

What we choose to *be* is always more important than what we choose to *do*.

# Success depends on backbone, not wishbone.

■■■

*Then you will have success if you are careful to observe the decrees and laws that the Lord gave Moses for Israel. Be strong and courageous. Do not be afraid or discouraged.*

1 Chronicles 22:13

During a baseball game in September 1974, Tommy John ruptured a ligament in his elbow. At the time, he was the leading pitcher in the National League. He appeared to be well on his way to a twenty-win season, and his team was on its way to the World Series. When he asked his surgeon if he had any chance of pitching again, he was told, "One in a hundred."

Shortly after his operation, his arm in a cast, he and his wife and baby daughter went to church. The sermon that morning was about Abraham and his wife Sarah, who was well into her seventies before she became pregnant with Isaac. John recalls that the minister looked right at him as he said, "You know, with God, nothing is impossible." That was all John needed to hear to encourage him to believe for a comeback. Sixteen weeks later, the cast came off and John started daily rehab. Recovery progressed inch by inch. It was a great day when he could finally bend his little finger to touch his thumb.

Then finally, after a year and a half of constant work and much pain, the day came when Tommy John walked back onto the mound. He pitched more games after his surgery than before it, and eventually pitched in the World Series.[15]

Choose to look today at the Source of your strength. With Him, all things are possible.

# Half the failures in life arise from pulling in one's horse as he is leaping.

■■■

*Jesus replied, "No one who puts his hand to the plow and looks back is fit for service in the kingdom of God."*

Luke 9:62

On a foggy morning in July of 1952, Florence Chadwick waded into the waters off of Catalina Island, intending to swim the channel to the California coast. An experienced long-distance swimmer, she had been the first woman to swim the English Channel in both directions.

The water was numbingly cold that day, and the fog was so thick she could hardly see the boats that accompanied her, in part, to keep sharks at bay. Several times she heard rifles being fired at the sharks she sensed in the inky waters with her. She swam for more than fifteen hours before asking to be lifted from the water. Her trainer encouraged her to swim on, telling her they were close to land. When Florence looked ahead, however, all she could see was fog. She quit — only a half mile from her goal.

Later she said, "I'm not excusing myself, but if I would have seen the land, I might have made it." It wasn't the cold, fear, or exhaustion that caused her to fail in her attempt to swim the Catalina Channel. It was the fog.[16]

Even if your goal isn't clearly in sight, press on. God hasn't brought you this far for you to fail. He is there in your future, and so is your reward.

Success in life is a matter not so much of talent or opportunity as of concentration and perseverance.

■■■

*Let us not get tired of doing what is right, for after a while we will reap a harvest of blessing if we don't get discouraged and give up.*

Galatians 6:9 TLB

Charles Schwab, one of the first presidents of Bethlehem Steel Company, once told efficiency expert Ivy Lee, "If you can give us something to pep us up to do the things we ought to do, I'll gladly pay you anything you ask within reason."

"Fine," Lee said, "I can give you something in twenty minutes that will step up your 'doing' by at least 50 percent." He then handed Schwab a piece of paper and said, "Write down the six most important tasks you have to do tomorrow and number them in the order of their importance." Then Lee said, "Now put this paper in your pocket and first thing tomorrow morning look at item one and start working on it until it is finished. Then tackle item two in the same way; then item three and so on. Do this until quitting time.... Do this every working day. After you've convinced yourself of the value of this system, have your men try it...and then send me a check for what you think it is worth." A few weeks later Schwab sent Lee a check for $25,000, calling his advice the most profitable lesson he had ever learned.

In just five years, Lee's plan was largely responsible for turning Bethlehem Steel Company into the biggest independent steel producer in the world.[17]

What are the six most important tasks you have to do tomorrow?

# There is a close correlation between getting up in the morning and getting up in the world.

■■■

*A little sleep, a little slumber, a little folding of the hands to rest — and poverty will come on you like a bandit and scarcity like an armed man.*

Proverbs 6:10,11

Award-winning figure skater Erin Sutton, 13, and world-class figure skater Brian Boitano have something in common: a love for ice skating and an intense dedication to their sport. Both also know a great deal about getting up before dawn in order to put in hours of practice on the ice.

Erin has been skating since she was four years old. As an eighth-grader, her "workday" on the ice began at 5:30 a.m. Even on Saturday mornings she was usually at the rink by 6:30. Boitano also knew that schedule as a young skater. For years, he skated from 5 to 10 a.m. before going to school. His dedication paid off. In 1988 he won Olympic gold, and in 1995 he was the professional world champion.

Being a champion hasn't changed Boitano's schedule a great deal. He is still at the ice rink before sunrise each day to practice for the competitive figure-skating season. Whether a skater is a veteran or a novice, it takes months of work to produce the three- to five-minute routines of leaps, spins, and intricate footwork that keep fans on the edge of their seats, and judges awarding high scores.[18]

If you want to be a champion, there are no shortcuts.

# I make progress by having people around me who are smarter than I am — and listening to them.

■■■

*Let the wise also hear and gain in learning.*

Proverbs 1:5 NRSV

Top corporate executives base the vast majority of their decisions upon information that is fed to them up through the ranks of workers, managers, and vice-presidents.

Head coaches frequently rely upon their assistant coaches to do the daily work of helping players improve their game and practice drills.

Military generals and admirals make decisions based upon the intelligence information gathered by those who are often of much lower rank.

Each of us relies upon others to have input into our lives so that we might make wise decisions and display sound moral behavior.

A very mature college freshman once said to her academic advisor, "Please tell me who the best professors are so I can take their courses." The advisor smiled and replied, "But shouldn't you be more concerned about getting the courses you need to complete your major?" The young woman replied, "I think if I start taking classes from the best professors, I'll know better what major I want!"

Surround yourself with people of excellent character who are well-trained, and are willing to give you their best advice. You'll advance much faster by listening more and talking less.

# Success is being able to come home, lay your head on the pillow and sleep in peace.

■■■

*His peace will keep your thoughts and hearts quiet and at rest as you trust in Christ Jesus.*

Philippians 4:7 TLB

Wess Roberts, in *Straight A's Never Made Anybody Rich,* tells of a young couple named Frank and Sally who were married two weeks after they graduated from college, then moved back to their home town to buy the general store owned by Frank's parents. He says, "Frank and Sally aren't glamorous, as people who make big time buyouts in corporate America may be.... What Frank and Sally wanted was to make it on their own in a familiar environment. Although the risks were greater, so was the potential reward. Over the years, they have expanded the dry goods side of the store and gained a regional reputation for Frank's butchering skills. They've had some close calls trying to pay bills on time, but they've survived.

Frank and Sally have three children. Frank has been on the town council for a number of years and Sally twice served on the school board. Their children work with them in the store on weekends and after school. As Roberts says, "Neither Frank nor Sally has ever seen the Manhattan skyline or taken the Lexington Avenue Express from Grand Central Station to Wall Street. But there are folks in New York who have never caught a rainbow trout or walked across town at night without fear."[19]

No one's life is perfect. But sometimes just living in peace is the greatest success a family can know.

# You've got to continue to grow, or you're just like last night's cornbread — stale and dry.

■■■

*Be careful so you will not fall from your strong faith, but grow in the grace and knowledge of our Lord and Savior Jesus Christ.*

2 Peter 3:17,18 NCV

George Burns probably knew more public acclaim in the last half of his life than he did during the first half. He strongly believed it was never too late to move ahead.

One of Burns' biggest breaks came at the death of one of his best friends, Jack Benny, who had been signed to play the lead with Walter Matthau in the movie version of "The Sunshine Boys," by Neil Simon. Burns' agent suggested Burns take the part. Says Burns, "At that time I was in my eighties and more or less semi-retired...I hadn't done a movie in 35 years. The film people were afraid that because of my age I'd forget my lines and it would slow down production of the film, but Irving convinced them to give me the role."

About a week before starting production, the director called for a reading of the screenplay with the members of the cast. Burns showed up without his manuscript. Both the director and producer were concerned that Burns' memory had failed him to the point he had forgotten his script. To everyone's surprise, Burns had already memorized all of his lines — as well as those of every other cast member! He won an Academy Award as Best Supporting Actor for his role in "The Sunshine Boys" and went on to do more than ten more movies.[20]

It's never too late and you're never too old!

# It's not enough to get all the breaks. You've got to know how to use them.

■■■

*He who gathers crops in summer is a wise son, but he who sleeps during harvest is a disgraceful son.*

Proverbs 10:5

Shortly after moving into a new home a number of years ago, a family was besieged by salesmen offering everything from laundry service to life insurance. One busy day a dairyman came to their door. "No," the woman of the house said firmly, "my husband and I don't drink milk."

"I'd be glad to deliver a quart every morning for cooking," the salesman said. "That's more than I need," she replied, starting to close the door. "Well, ma'am, how about some cream? Berries comin' in now, and...." She said curtly, "No, we never use cream."

The dairyman slowly retreated and the woman congratulated herself on her sales resistance. The fact was, she had already ordered from another dairy and she had simply taken the easy way out. The next morning, however, the same dairyman appeared at her door, a bowl of dewy ripe strawberries held carefully in one hand and a half-pint bottle of cream in the other. "Lady," he said, as he poured the cream over the berries and handed them to her, "I got to thinkin' — you sure have missed a lot!" Needless to say, she switched dairies.[21]

You haven't exhausted all of your opportunities until you've tapped all your creativity — and creativity is an inexhaustible resource!

# Success that is easy is cheap.

■■■

*He is a rewarder of those who diligently seek Him.*

Hebrews 11:6 NKJV

In *The Seven Habits of Highly Successful People,* Stephen Covey tells about a small computer software company that had developed new software, which it sold on a five-year contract to a bank. The bank president was excited about the product and his people were highly supportive. A month later, though, the bank changed presidents. The new president said he wanted to back out of the deal.

The president of the computer company knew his own company was in financial trouble. He knew he had every legal right to enforce the contract, but he also knew the right thing to do. He told the bank president, "We have a contract. Your bank has secured our products and services to convert you to this new software program. But we understand that you're not happy about it. So what we'd like to do is give you back the contract, give you back your deposit, and if you are ever looking for a software solution in the future, come back and see us." In doing this, he was walking away from an $84,000 contract. It was nearly financial suicide for his company. However, three months later, the new bank president called to say, "I'm now going to make changes in my data processing, and I want to do business with you." They signed a contract worth $240,000.[22]

Who says nice guys always finish last?

# A purpose is the eternal condition of success.

■■■

*Where there is no vision,*
*the people perish.*

Proverbs 29:18 KJV

If I can throw a single ray of light across the darkened pathway of another; if I can aid some soul to clearer sight of life and duty, and thus bless my brother; if I can wipe from any human cheek a tear, I shall not have lived my life in vain while here.

If I can guide some erring one to truth, inspire within his heart a sense of duty; if I can plant within my soul of rosy youth a sense of right, a love of truth and beauty; if I can teach one man that God and heaven are near, I shall not then have lived in vain while here.

If from my mind I banish doubt and fear, and keep my life attuned to love and kindness; if I can scatter light and hope and cheer, and help remove the curse of mental blindness; if I can make more joy, more hope, less pain, I shall not have lived and loved in vain.

If by life's roadside I can plant a tree, beneath whose shade some wearied head may rest, though I may never share its beauty, I shall yet be truly blest — though no one knows my name, nor drops a flower upon my grave, I shall not have lived in vain while here.[23]

— Unknown

There is a reason for your life today. As you discover it, you will have a purpose for living. As you fulfill it, you will be able to call today successful.

# Ninety-nine percent of failures come from people who have the habit of making excuses.

■■■

*But they all alike began to make excuses.... I tell you, not one of those men who were invited will get a taste of my banquet.*

Luke 14:18,24

"You see, God, it's like this: We could attend church more faithfully if your day came at some other time. You have chosen a day that comes at the end of a hard week, and we're all tired out. Not only that, but it's the day following Saturday night, and Saturday night is one time when we feel that we should go out and enjoy ourselves. Often it is after midnight when we reach home, and it is almost impossible to get up on Sunday morning. And you must realize that you have picked the very day on which the morning paper takes the longest to read — the day when the biggest meal of the week must be prepared. We'd like to go to church, and know that we should; but you have just chosen the wrong day."

This tongue-in-cheek excuse for poor church attendance speaks well of the excuses we use to justify our unproductive behavior. Many of us need to own up to the fact that we are not succeeding because of our own laziness, errors, or lack of vision.

Charles W. Morton, an editor for *Atlantic Monthly*, once wrote about a Harvard freshman who came to the Dean's office to explain his tardiness in handing in an assignment. "I'm sorry, sir, but I was not feeling very well." The dean replied, "Young man, please bear in mind that by far the greater part of the world's work is carried on by people who are not feeling very well."[24]

# There is in this world no such force as the force of a man determined to rise.

■■■

*Let us lay aside every weight,*
*and the sin which so easily ensnares us,*
*and let us run with endurance*
*the race that is set before us.*

Hebrews 12:1 NKJV

At age eighteen, Arthur Farquhar read about some big-business leaders and decided he would like to know more about them and get their advice before he started work as a machinist.

Early one morning, he made his way into New York City. Ignorant of city office hours, he went directly to William B. Astor's office at seven o'clock. A clerk was already at work in the outer office. In an adjoining room, Farquhar saw a heavy-set man he instantly recognized as being Mr. Astor. Mr. Astor asked Arthur what he wanted. He replied, "I want to know how to make a million dollars." Astor saw initiative in the boy and talked to him for an hour. He also recommended a list of other men to visit and Farquhar proceeded to call upon them — leading merchants, editors, and bankers.

In the end, the advice he received about how to make money didn't help much. But his acquaintance with men who had succeeded gave him models to imitate and the confidence he needed to try. He adopted their work habits. Within two years, he was a partner in the shop where he had started as an apprentice. By age twenty-four, he was the sole proprietor of a farm-machinery business, from which he made more than his million dollars, although his plant was twice destroyed by fire.[25]

How determined are you to reach your goals?

# To have grown wise and kind is real success.

■■■

*Therefore, as God's chosen,*
*set apart and enjoying His love,*
*clothe yourselves with tenderness of*
*heart, kindliness, humility,*
*gentleness, patient endurance.*

Colossians 3:12 MLB

John Ehrlichman, one of those convicted in the Watergate scandals of the early 1970s, has written that upon his release from prison, he found himself at a very low ebb. He began to take stock of his life: "Every day I read the Bible, walked on the beach, and sat in front of my fireplace thinking and sketching, with no outline or agenda. I had no idea where all this was leading or what answers I'd find. Most of the time I didn't even know what the questions were. I just watched and listened. I was wiped out. I had nothing left that had been of value to me — honor, credibility, virtue, recognition, profession — nor did I have the allegiance of my family. I had managed to lose that too.

"Since about 1975 I have begun to learn to see myself. I care what I perceive about my integrity, my capacity to love and be loved, and my essential worth.... Those interludes, the Nixon episodes in my life, have ended. In a paradoxical way, I'm grateful for them. Somehow I had to see all of that and grow to understand it in order to arrive at the place where I find myself now."[26]

The tragedies of our lives are sometimes the best catalysts to transform us into people whom God can use. Strength of character is truly the highest success a person can achieve.

# Three qualities vital to success: toil, solitude, prayer.

■■■

*Do not let this Book of the Law depart from your mouth; meditate on it day and night, so that you may be careful to do everything written in it. Then you will be prosperous and successful.*

Joshua 1:8

Charles G. Finney, a young apprentice lawyer, was sitting in a small-town law office in the state of New York early one morning. He was all alone when he sensed the Lord speaking to him.

"Finney, what are you going to do when you finish your course?" He said, "Put out a shingle and practice law."

"Then what?" He replied, "Get rich."

"Then what?" He said, "Retire."

"Then what?" "Die."

"Then what?" And he spoke his next words with a tremble in his voice, "The judgment."

Finney left the office immediately and ran for the woods a half mile away. He prayed there all day and vowed that he would not leave until he had made peace with God. He had studied law for four years, but he emerged from the woods that evening with the high purpose of living to the glory of God and enjoying Him forever. God began to use him in a mighty way, not as a lawyer, but as a preacher. He brought thousands of people to a conversion experience over the next fifty years of his life.[27]

Any career can be a way of bringing glory to God, as long as you know you are working to further His kingdom, and not simply to build one of your own.

There is not a man that has not "his hour," and there is not a thing that has not its place.

■■■

*There is an appointed time for everything. And there is a time for every event under heaven.*

Ecclesiastes 3:1 NASB

Los Angeles Dodger Brett Butler believes in miracles. In fact, he believes he is one. After playing a baseball game against Colorado in May of 1996, Butler thought he was only going to have his tonsils out. He planned to miss about three weeks of playing time. The surgeons, however, found that he had cancer. The news hit Butler hard. He recalls, "I said to myself, 'My God, I'm thirty-eight years old and I'm going to die.'" His mother had died of cancer a year before. After the initial shock wore off, he chose to respond with faith, instead of fear. He underwent two operations and thirty-two radiation treatments, determined to return to the Dodgers before the season ended. Few thought he could do it.

Butler, however, said, "I want people to know that I felt their prayers, and I felt their love. I believe God answers prayer. I want to acknowledge that in some capacity. This is an opportunity to show...I am a disciple for Jesus. Now I'll be able to measure my success from the lowness of my career." On September 6, Butler was once again on the playing field wearing his Los Angeles Dodgers uniform. He went 1-for-3 with a walk, a run scored, and two nice catches to help his team win the game.[28]

Every event in your life has some purpose in molding you into the person God desires for you to be.

# Success is more a function of consistent common sense than it is of genius.

■■■

*Commit your work to the Lord, then it will succeed.*

Proverbs 16:3 TLB

In 1987, the Gallup Organization probed the attitudes and traits of 1500 prominent people selected at random from *Who's Who in America*. They were looking for a combination of traits that might be considered a "success personality." The most prevalent quality possessed by those who responded was common sense!

Some 79 percent of those polled received a top score in this category and 61 percent said common sense was "very important" to their success.

To most, common sense means the ability to render sound, practical judgments on everyday affairs. Generally, to do this, one must have the ability to move directly to the core of a matter. One of those polled, a Texas oil and gas executive, said, "The key ability for success is *simplifying*. In conducting meetings and dealing with industry regulators, reducing a complex problem to the simplest terms is highly important."[29]

Can common sense be learned or are you born with it? Most believe it can be developed. We learn it by observing it in others, and learning from their mistakes. We can hone our common sense by forcing ourselves to state what we believe in concise terms, even if we are the only audience for what we say or write.

Success is not predestined. Sometimes it just takes plain old common sense.

# When you make a mistake, admit it; learn from it and don't repeat it.

■■■

*Godly sorrow brings repentance that leads to salvation and leaves no regret.*

2 Corinthians 7:10

In 1736, at the age of twenty-six, John Wesley sailed from England to Georgia to preach to the Indians. Two years later he wrote in his journal: "I went to America to convert the Indians; but O! who shall convert me?" Wesley's honest recognition of the weakness of his faith led him on a spiritual search. Soon afterward, he went to a meeting in Aldersgate Street, London, an event at which his heart was "strangely warmed" as he made a fresh commitment of his life to Christ. It was after this that Wesley was successful in leading thousands to accept Christ through his energetic and tireless preaching.[30]

It is very often only when we truly admit to ourselves our failures, that we can begin to see what we must do to change our ways and become successful.

It is only when we admit we are weak that we put ourselves into a position to find strength, or to accept help from others.

It is only when we admit something isn't working that we can stand back and determine what has gone wrong, what needs to be fixed, and how to fix it.

As long as we think of ourselves as perfect, right, justified, or strong, we will not seek out ways in which to grow or change.

# Success won at the cost of self-respect is not success.

■■■

*For what will a man be profited,*
*if he gains the whole world,*
*and forfeits his soul?*

Matthew 16:26 NASB

In *Sin, Sex, and Self-Control,* Norman Vincent Peale tells of an incident in the life of a writer he knew, a man who specialized in writing medical articles for popular magazines. He told Peale he had received a check for $1500 from the public relations representative of a large pharmaceutical company in the mail. The public relations man wanted the writer to mention favorably the products of his company. He said if this could be arranged, other checks would follow. The writer said, "The silly thing about all this was that I was occasionally mentioning this fellow's products quite legitimately. So he was trying to bribe me to do something I was already doing. And believe me, I needed the money. But somehow I couldn't quite bring myself to cash the check. It lay on my desk, day after day, and my work went very badly. Finally, somewhere, I found the courage to send it back. I knew that if I kept it I would be selling my independence and my integrity. And this was something I couldn't afford to do." Almost immediately his work began to get better.

He said, "It was just as if a big wave of energy came out of nowhere and gave my typewriter wings. In less than a week, I wrote two complete articles — and made almost as much money anyway!"[31]

Character can be sold out; however, it cannot be purchased.

# One important key to success is self-confidence. An important key to self-confidence is preparation.

■■■

*Study to show thyself approved unto God, a workman that needeth not to be ashamed, rightly dividing the word of truth.*

2 Timothy 2:15 KJV

In the 1984 Olympics, heavyweight boxer Henry Tillman planned out a very careful strategy. He decided he would fight defensively, simply warding off his opponent's blows, until he saw an opening for a strike of his own. Minutes into the fight, it became obvious to Tillman that his opponent had planned the same strategy! After the bell sounded ending the first round, Tillman stepped back, dropped his hands, and mentally shifted gears. He recognized that his initial game plan might not work, but he had come prepared with a second plan. He switched to a take-the-offensive mode of fighting, won the match, and ultimately won a gold medal.

Figure skater Kristi Yamaguchi also had a "plan B" for her Olympic bid. Originally, she had planned to perform her most difficult jump — three revolutions in the air and a graceful single-skate landing known as the triple salchow. A slight stumble in the early portion of her routine led her to make a change. She cut the triple salchow to a double, regained her balance, caught up with her music, and then went on to perform another triple jump — the lutz.[32]

No matter how much we rehearse or plan, things don't always go as we desire. True champions are those who are prepared to adapt if necessary and switch to what works.

# Six essential qualities that are the key to success: sincerity, personal integrity, humility, courtesy, wisdom, charity.

■■■

*Do your best to improve your faith. You can do this by adding goodness, understanding, self-control, patience, devotion to God, concern for others, and love.... If you keep on doing this, you won't stumble or fall.*

2 Peter 1:5-7,10 CEV

When William was only sixteen years old, he left home to seek his fortune. He tied all his possessions into a bundle that he could carry in his hand. He told an old canal-boat captain that his father was too poor to keep him and the only trade he knew was soap and candle making.

The old captain knelt and earnestly prayed for the boy, then advised him, "Someone will soon be the leading soap-maker in New York. It can be you as well as someone else. Be a good man, give your heart to Christ, pay the Lord all that belongs to Him, make an honest soap; give a full pound, and I'm certain you'll be a prosperous and rich man."

When he arrived in the city, William remembered the captain's words and although poor and lonely, he joined a church and gave one-tenth of his first dollar, just as the captain had exhorted him to do. Once he gained regular employment, he soon became a partner, then later, sole owner of the business. He made an honest soap, and as he became more successful, he increased his giving from 10 percent to 50 percent, and finally to 100 percent of his income. In all, William Colgate gave millions.[33]

The marks of success are not only know-how and diligence, but humility and generosity.

# The simple virtues of willingness, readiness, alertness, and courtesy will carry a young man farther than mere smartness.

■■■

*The people blessed all the men who willingly offered themselves.*

Nehemiah 11:2 NKJV

Many years ago, an elderly man and his wife entered the lobby of a small Philadelphia hotel. "All the big places are filled," the man said. "Can you give us a room?" The clerk replied that with three conventions in town, no accommodations were available anywhere. "Every guest room is taken," he said, but then added, "but I can't send a nice couple like you out into the rain at one o'clock in the morning. Would you be willing to sleep in my room?"

The next morning as he paid his bill, the elderly man said to the clerk, "You are the kind of manager who should be the boss of the best hotel in the United States. Maybe someday I'll build one for you." The clerk laughed and forgot about the incident. About two years later, however, he received a letter containing a round-trip ticket to New York and a request that he be the guest of the elderly couple he had befriended.

Once in New York, the old man led the clerk to the corner of Fifth Avenue and Thirty-fourth Street, where he pointed to an incredible new building and declared, "That is the hotel I have just built for you to manage." The young man, George C. Boldt, accepted the offer of William Waldorf Astor to become the manager of the original Waldorf-Astoria, considered the finest hotel in the world in its time.[34]

In my vocabulary, there is no such word as "can't," because I recognize that my abilities are given to me by God to do what needs to be done.

■■■

*I can do everything God asks me to with the help of Christ who gives me the strength and power.*

Philippians 4:13 TLB

Tom Dooley was a young doctor who organized hospitals, raised money, and literally poured his life out in service to the afflicted people of Southeast Asia. In a letter he wrote these "I can, through Christ" words to the president of Notre Dame, his alma mater. He said, "They've got me down. Flat on the back, with plaster, sand bags, and hot water bottles. I've contrived a way of pumping the bed up a bit so that, with a long reach, I can get to my typewriter....Whenever my cancer acts up a bit, and it is certainly 'acting up' now, I turn inward. Less do I think of my hospitals around the world, or of 94 doctors, fund-raisers, and the like. More do I think of one Divine Doctor and my personal fund of grace. It has become pretty definite that the cancer has spread to the lumbar vertebra, accounting for all the back problems over the last two months. I have monstrous phantoms; all men do. And inside and outside the wind blows. But when the time comes, like now, then the storm around me does not matter. The winds within me do not matter. Nothing human or earthly can touch me. A peace gathers in my heart. What seems unpossessable, I can possess. What seems unfathomable, I can fathom. What is unutterable, I can utter. Because I can pray. I can communicate. How do people endure anything...if they cannot have God?"[35]

# The man who works for the gold in the job rather than for the money in the pay envelope is the fellow who gets on.

■■■

*In all the work you are doing, work the best you can. Work as if you were doing it for the Lord, not for people.*

Colossians 3:23 NCV

During the early days of World War II, an impeccably uniformed U.S. war correspondent, sporting an overdose of Aqua Velva cologne to ward off what he feared would be nauseating aromas, stepped warily into a primitive Chinese field hospital. Overcome almost immediately by the smell of the dead and dying, shocked at his response to the incoherent cries of the wounded, he hastily retreated in search of fresh air.

He walked right into one of the most stunning sights he had seen on his journey. A beautiful young nun, of the American-based Maryknoll order, was on her knees before a filthy Chinese soldier. She was patiently swabbing his gangrenous leg as he lay on a reeking mat. The correspondent turned his gaze away, repulsed.

"Sister," he said, "I wouldn't do that for a million dollars."

The nun paused only momentarily in her ministrations and said, "Neither would I."[36]

There are jobs that are far more valuable than the pay associated with them. They give opportunity for nobility of character and majesty of purpose to be exercised.

The man who will
use his skill and con-
structive imagination
to see how much
he can give for a dollar,
instead of how little
he can give for a dollar,
is bound to succeed.

■■■

*By your standard of measure, it shall be measured to you.*

Matthew 7:2 NASB

In July of 1938, Victor Gruen came to America from Austria with $8 in his pocket and an architect's T-square in his luggage. In his homeland, he had championed innovative public housing, and had just begun to get architectural commissions from Vienna's department stores when Hitler's armies invaded. He fled to the United States, bringing with him an idea inspired by the markets of medieval Austrian and Swiss towns, and by the stately Galleria Vittorio Emanuele II in Milan. He introduced the covered shopping mall to America.

Gruen's first mall opened in Minnesota in the mid-1950s. It was little more than a courtyard centered between two department stores. A single roof over the entire structure, however, meant that construction costs for smaller, individual stores could be reduced, making the entire complex cheaper to build.

So many developers hired Gruen that his firm soon had offices in six major cities. He was called in to redesign entire downtown areas, as well as to redesign the city of Tehran.[37]

Gruen's concept was an answer to a simple question — how much commerce can a person put under one roof? In your line of work, how might you give your customers more, without raising the price? Your innovation just may be the key to your success!

# The smile of God is victory.

■■■

*Do what is right and good in the sight of the Lord.*

Deuteronomy 6:18 NKJV

Eric Liddell ran every race to win, his eyes always on the finish line. He didn't seek fame, although he attained it. He ran out of a love for God and deep desire to give Him lasting glory. From his youth, he desired to take the Gospel to the people of northeast China. However, the 1908 Olympics, which were held in London, deeply impressed the young Scot. He gave in to the encouragement of friends and entered a local track competition. He beat the clear favorite, and immediately gained public recognition. One of Edinburgh University's finest athletic trainers offered Liddell his services. He prayed and decided to use his talent as a means of honoring its creator, God.

Liddell went to the 1924 Olympics known as the "Flying Scot." Unfortunately, he heard that the heats for his race, the 100-meter sprint, were to be held on a Sunday. He was disappointed, but he never doubted or questioned his decision *not* to run. The practice of honoring the Sabbath was sacred to him. He turned his attention to the 400-meter race, but no one thought he would finish in the medals. Sprinters rarely did well in middle-distance races. Liddell, however, believed the Scripture: "He that honors me, I will honor." He set both an Olympic record and a world record.[38]

Have you placed yourself in a position for God to honor *you?*

# 'Tis man's to fight, but Heaven's to give success.

■■■

*The Lord says, "Don't be afraid! Don't be paralyzed by this mighty army! For the battle is not yours, but God's!"*

2 Chronicles 20:15 TLB

Several years ago, the world watched in awe as media attention was focused on three gray whales that were ice-bound off Point Barrow, Alaska. Their battered bodies floated listlessly as they gasped for breath at a hole in the ice. Somehow they had become trapped in an ice pack before they could begin their annual migration. Their only hope for survival was to be transported five miles past the ice pack to the open sea.

Rescuers began cutting a string of breathing holes about twenty yards apart in the six-inch-thick ice. Then for eight days, they coaxed the whales from hole to hole, mile after mile. Along the way, one of the whales vanished, but the other two eventually swam to freedom.[39]

Are you feeling trapped under a heavy load today? Do you fear it may suffocate you? Do you seem to be far from the "open seas," or the free schedule you desire?

Identify where you want to be and then chart your course in a series of small steps or short-term goals. Take time for a breather, a bit of relaxation, as you reach each goal. God will lead you and help you toward any destination that is in keeping with His good desire for you, but you must make the effort to follow.

# To be a winner in life, we must first be a winner inside.

■■■

*Behold, You desire truth in the inward parts, and in the hidden part You will make me to know wisdom.*

Psalm 51:6 NKJV

In 1925, Herman Krannert was summoned to Chicago to have lunch with his company's president. While they were dining, the president said, "Herman, we're going to promote you...you're to be the newest member of the Board of Directors." Krannert was stunned and pleased until the president said, "As a member of the Board of Directors you will vote *exactly* the way I tell you to." Krannert was disappointed, and then angry. He finally said, "I will not be a puppet for anybody on a Board of Directors. Not only that, but I won't work for a company where such demands are made. I quit."

When he returned home that night, his wife was supportive of his decision, but he was still out of a job. Four nights later a knock came at his door. Six senior executives from the company came in, excited. "Herman, we heard what happened the other day. We think that's the greatest thing we've ever heard. In fact, we quit too."

The six men then announced, "We're going to work for you." "How are you going to work for me?" Krannert stammered, "I don't even have a job!" That night the seven of them sat down at Krannert's dining room table and created the Inland Container Corporation, which became a corporate empire.[40]

In doing the right thing, we find the right path.

It is sheer waste of time to imagine what I would do if things were different. They are not different.

■■■

*Brothers, I do not consider myself yet to have taken hold of it. But one thing I do: Forgetting what is behind and straining toward what is ahead.*

Philippians 3:13

In 1980, the Pacific Northwest shuddered under the devastating force of the Mount Saint Helens eruption. Forests were annihilated by fire. Rivers were choked with debris. Fish and wildlife were destroyed. The air became toxic. Reporters ominously echoed predictions that acid rain clouds would form and the world's weather patterns could be permanently changed. The future for the area seemed bleak.

Nevertheless, less than a year after the eruption, scientists studying the area discovered that in spite of the fact that the rivers had been clogged with hot mud, volcanic ash, and floating debris, the salmon and steelhead had miraculously managed to survive by swimming *alternate* streams home to spawn. Some of the waterways through which they had swum were less than six inches deep, barely enough water to cover their bodies.

Within a few short years, fields, lakes, and rivers surrounding Mount Saint Helens teemed with life. The water and soil actually seemed to be *enriched* by nutrients supplied by the exploding volcano.[41]

Trouble usually doesn't last forever. It may be the means to show you a different way to go, a different way to live. It may be an opportunity to start afresh. Challenges in life can enrich us and make us stronger. God's creation, including man, was designed to overcome!

# The surest way not to fail is to determine to succeed.

■■■

*Choose for yourselves this day whom you will serve.*

Joshua 24:15 NKJV

When Arago, the astronomer, was young, he became thoroughly discouraged in his study of mathematics. One day he noticed a few words written on the flyleaf of a textbook. The words were by the famous D'Alembert, who apparently had once been as discouraged as he was. He wrote, "Go on, sir, go on!"

Later, Arago said that this one sentence was the best teacher of mathematics he ever had. He followed this advice doggedly until he became the leading mathematician of his day.[42]

A family that had spent weeks crossing the plains in their covered wagon, finally began their descent from the Sierra Nevada mountains into the valley of California. They reflected back upon their journey as they stared at the beauty in front of them. "Did you think we would make it?" one man asked another as he recounted the litany of broken wagon wheels, Indian scares, dangerous river crossings, and shortage of supplies they had experienced. The other man replied, "I didn't dare think we wouldn't. I figured the minute I thought we might not make it, I'd stop and stay at that spot the rest of my life. And I didn't see any place I wanted to stay!"

You've got to keep moving if you ever hope to arrive someplace other than where you are presently.

# The only thing that stops you is yourself. Period.

■■■

*Create in me a pure heart, O God, and renew a steadfast spirit within me.*

Psalm 51:10

David Rabin was only forty-five when he was diagnosed with ALS, which is also known as Lou Gehrig's disease. The disease causes gradual paralysis throughout the body and there is no treatment or cure. Rabin, a professor of medicine at Vanderbilt University, knew well the progression of the disease. He says that when he first learned of the disease in medical school, "none frightened me more."

Rabin was determined, however, to continue to live and work as normally as possible. When he could no longer examine patients, he served as a consultant. When he could no longer get to the hospital, laboratory teams came to his home for regular conferences. In this way, he was able to direct an active research program.

When he could no longer turn the pages of a book with his hands, he got a machine that turned the pages automatically. When he lost his voice, he found a computer that became a vehicle for both speaking and writing — it operates on impulses from eyebrow muscles. He has said, "I talk to my family — that is most wonderful. I can make conversation with friends...I can work independently again...and I am able to interact with the persons in my laboratory."[43]

As long as there is a will, there is nearly always a way.

# It is the amount and excellence of what is over and above the required that determines the greatness of ultimate distinction.

■■■

*Having confidence in your obedience, I write to you, knowing that you will do even more than I say.*

Philemon 1:21 NKJV

In 1769 Mary Ludwig, daughter of a Dutch dairyman, was sent to Carlisle, Pennsylvania, to become a domestic servant in the home of a doctor. A few months later, not yet sixteen, she married a barber named John Hays. When Hays enlisted in the Pennsylvania artillery, Mary followed her husband's outfit, washing and cooking for the soldiers.

In the summer of 1778, the American army was pursuing British troops and they met at the Battle of Monmouth. It was a blistering hot day and fifty soldiers died of thirst during the battle. Not content to stay back in the camp, Mary braved the gunshots and cannon fire to carry water from a stream to the parched American troops. This brave act earned Mary her legendary nickname, "Molly Pitcher."

As the battle wore on, Mary saw her husband fall wounded next to his cannon. His commanding officer ordered the cannon pulled back from the front lines, but Mary, who had watched her husband in training, stepped into his place and kept firing for the rest of the battle. In the end, the battle ended as a draw, but Mary won the admiration of the other soldiers, who called her "Sergeant Molly." Legend has it that General Washington himself gave her a noncommissioned title and made up songs about her.[44]

Extra effort above and beyond the expected never goes unnoticed or unrewarded by God.

The young man who would succeed must identify his interests with those of his employer and exercise the same diligence in matters entrusted to him as he would in his own affairs.

■■■

*And if ye have not been faithful in that which is another man's, who shall give you that which is your own?*

Luke 16:12 KJV

When Greg was twelve, he worked summers at his father's small brick-cleaning business. He still remembers that if he fell short of the company standards, he had to stay late until he got it right. His father wasn't mean — he demanded the same high standards of himself. When Greg was seventeen, he married and moved out of his parents' home into a housing project known for drug trafficking and gang violence. Some of Greg's friends went to jail, others were killed. Nobody gave his marriage to Verlyn, age fifteen, a chance. They believed in each other, however, and worked hard to succeed.

Greg was working at Southwest Super Foods, where he was promoted from bagger to stock clerk. He took pride in lining up cans and keeping the shelves dusted and the floors swept. By the 1980s, he had become the stock manager. He then joined the Hudson-Thompson Company chain. In 1983, his new company sent him to manage one of their unprofitable stores — the very store where he had started as a bagger sixteen years earlier.

A year later, he and Verlyn took a risk and bought the store. He turned the failing sales around, then began to look for other stores to buy. By 1995, they owned eight stores with a total revenue of $52 million a year. He has never forgotten his father's advice — good for any success-bound person: each job is like a signature, and your name is only as good as the quality of work you do.[45]

# To become an able and successful man in any profession, three things are necessary: nature, study, and practice.

■■■

*Be a good workman, one who does not need to be ashamed when God examines your work. Know what his Word says and means.*

2 Timothy 2:15 TLB

In 1988, K. Anders Ericsson of Florida State University in Tallahassee and colleagues of his in Germany, compared the careers of two groups of young musicians. The ten members of the first group were identified as potential world-class international performers. A second group of ten was identified as merely good. Ericsson also took a look at ten violinists who regularly performed in orchestras of international reputation, such as the Berlin Philharmonic. Both student groups kept diaries of their practice schedules, and all three groups provided estimates of their schedules previous to the study.

Of the student musicians, Ericsson found that by age 20, the "good" group had practiced 7500 hours, but the potential top-flight performers had practiced 10,000 hours — the equivalent of more than a year of hard work. The top group's total practice time almost exactly matched that of the symphony performers at the same age.[46]

Keeping your nose to the grindstone in mindless drudgery only causes pain. It's not just a matter of putting in hours alone. It's also a matter of what kind of effort you put into the hours. But, if you put in a good effort every time you practice your talent or hone your skill, the more hours you practice, the greater your rewards will be down the line.

If you wish success in life, make *perseverance* your bosom friend, *experience* your wise counselor, *caution* your elder brother, and *hope* your guardian genius.

■■■

*Knowing that tribulation brings about perseverance; and perseverance, proven character; and proven character, hope; and hope does not disappoint.*

Romans 5:3-5 NASB

One day, after long hours of water-skiing, teenage Todd Houston was untangling the ski ropes. The gears of the ski boat kicked unexpectedly into reverse, and his legs were sucked into its propellers. In a moment's time, both legs were severely injured. Doctors said there was little chance he would ever walk again. Todd slowly recovered from his wounds, but bone disease eventually set into his right foot, and in 1981, he faced amputation. He recalls that just prior to the surgery, a wave of calmness swept over him. He recalled a Bible verse he had learned as a child, "Righteousness goes before him and prepares the way for his steps."

Todd went on to finish college with honors. Fitted with an artificial leg, he could walk, but not much more. Then in 1993, he acquired a new prosthesis called Flex-Foot. With hard work, he was soon able to run twelve miles a day! Then he heard of an organization that was looking for an amputee to climb the highest mountain in each of the fifty states. Mountain climbing is dangerous, even with two good legs, but Todd was cautious and persistent, and on August 7, 1994, he had climbed all fifty high points and had set a world record in the process.[47]

In all his experiences, Todd Houston has used a winning mix of perseverance, experience, caution, and hope. You can too!

The worst bankrupt in the world is the man who has lost his enthusiasm. Let a man lose everything else in the world but his enthusiasm and he will come through again to success.

■■■

*It is fine to be zealous, provided the purpose is good, and to be so always.*

Galatians 4:18

Former Atomic Energy Commission chairman Gordon Dean wrote the following list of "Lessons Learned" — most of which express an attitude of abundance toward life:

1. Never lose your capacity for enthusiasm.

2. Never lose your capacity for indignation.

3. Never judge people, don't type them too quickly; but in a pinch never first assume that a man is bad; first assume always he is good and at worst he is in the gray area between bad and good.

4. Never be impressed by wealth alone, or thrown by poverty.

5. If you can't be generous when it's hard to be, you won't be when it's easy.

6. The greatest builder of confidence is the ability to do something — almost anything — well.

7. When that confidence comes, then strive for humility; you aren't as good as all that.

8. The way to become truly useful is to seek the best that other brains have to offer. Use them to supplement your own, and be prepared to give credit to them when they have helped.

9. The greatest tragedies in world and personal events stem from misunderstandings — communicate.[48]

Do not attempt to do a thing unless you are sure of yourself; but do not relinquish it simply because someone else is not sure of you.

■■■

*In quietness and confidence shall be your strength.*

Isaiah 30:15 NKJV

At age sixty-five, the veteran of many battles in the world of business, a man walked into the office of a large company that sold optical goods. He was told, "At present, there's no opening that a man of your experience...." He interrupted, "I can take on almost anything. I can sell. I've been selling for half a century." The president of the company relented and said, "There's a possible spot in Maryland. We have a part-time man who's turned in only a couple of hundred dollars' worth of business in the past month. Maybe you could better that." The old man said, "When do I leave?" He was on the 8:40 plane.

A few days later, orders began to come in from the new salesman in Maryland. The initial trickle of orders swelled to a flood, more than ten thousand dollars' worth in one day, five thousand dollars more the next, and so on. It was obvious the old man had lost his mind, they decided. The firm just didn't do business on such a scale. Nobody took them seriously. And then, the telegrams and phone calls began to pour in from retail stores. Where were their shipments?

Within a year, the man became vice-president in charge of the sales staff. He became the much-loved grandfather of the firm.[49]

Others will find it much easier to believe in you if you believe in yourself.

# The worst use that can be made of success is to boast of it.

■■■

*As has been written,*
*"Let the boaster boast in the Lord."*
1 Corinthians 1:31 MLB

Few people have the privilege of a private audience with Pope John Paul II. NBC News' Washington bureau chief, Tim Russert, is one of those few. The "Meet the Press" moderator was sent to attempt to convince His Holiness that it was in his interest to appear on the "Today" show. As a former altar boy, however, Russert found his Catholic heritage overshadowing his professional motivation.

He has said, "I'll never forget it. My thoughts soon turned away from NBC's ratings toward the idea of salvation. As I stood there with the Vicar of Christ, I simply blurted, 'Bless me, Father!'

"He put his arm around my shoulder and whispered, 'You are the one called Timothy, the man from NBC?'

"I said, 'Yes, yes, that's me.'

"'They tell me you're a very important man.'

"Taken aback, I said, 'Your Holiness, there are only two of us in this room, and I am certainly a distant second.' He looked at me and said, 'Right.'"[50]

Ultimately, the most any of us can say about our accomplishments and possessions is this, "God has allowed me to have this for a brief time on the earth." All that we do is fleeting. It is who we become in Christ Jesus that lasts forever.

Aim at perfection in everything, though in most things it is unattainable; however, they who aim at it, and persevere, will come much nearer to it, than those whose laziness and despondency make them give it up as unattainable.

■■■

*You are to be perfect, even as your Father in heaven is perfect.*

Matthew 5:48 TLB

One of the areas of life in which nearly all of us can improve, is in the management of our time. Time management is critical for maximizing daily work, the cornerstone of achievement. It is vital to accomplishing all that we desire.

Debra Smith of the Dible Management Development Seminar organization has presented these seven classic techniques for making the most of each day:

1. Complete daily priorities — central concerns and essentials first.

2. Group related activities together in order to save time, as well as create more time.

3. Divide big tasks into workable steps, which also helps to maintain confidence.

4. Construct a timetable for every project.

5. For maximum results, concentrate on, and complete, one step at a time.

6. To maintain a high energy level, finish each task thoroughly.

7. To prevent procrastination — "do it now."

A day in which you manage your time well, in line with your values and priorities, is a day that can rightly be labeled successful.[51]

Never one thing and seldom one person can make for a success. It takes a number of them merging into one perfect whole.

■■■

*Under his direction the whole body is fitted together perfectly, and each part in its own special way helps the other parts, so that the whole body is healthy and growing and full of love.*

Ephesians 4:16 TLB

The Malcolm Baldridge National Quality Award is the highest honor attainable by an American company. To win, a company must convince a blue-ribbon panel that it produces the highest quality products in the nation. In 1988, sixty-six companies competed for the award. The winner was Motorola — the entire company, not just a division.

Motorola actually began its quest for the award in 1981. Teams were sent to outstanding organizations around the world to learn how Motorola might improve its manufacturing performance. Employees were challenged to drastically reduce the number of defects in their work. Hourly workers were made responsible for identifying mistakes, and were rewarded for doing so. Engineers were able to reduce the number of parts in a cellular phone from 1,378 to 523. The result of all this effort was the manufacturing of cellular phones that were 99.9997 percent defect-free.

By involving the entire company, morale was increased tremendously. And because Motorola was able to save $250 million by eliminating costly repairs and replacements, their revenue increased 23 percent, and profits rose 44 percent — an all-time record high. All of which translated into higher wages and better benefits.[52]

Success is a team effort. When everyone participates, everyone wins!

# Snowflakes are one of nature's most fragile things, but just look what they can do when they stick together.

■■■

*Let us not give up meeting together, as some are in the habit of doing, but let us encourage one another.*

Hebrews 10:25

As part of a leadership training program, a class of about fifty people was given a challenge: feed breakfast to 1,000 homeless people in downtown Los Angeles and acquire clothing to give away without spending a dime of their own money. They were given the challenge on Thursday and expected to carry it out on Saturday! No one in the group was in the catering business or had ever done anything like it. They all felt it was a monumental challenge!

Almost immediately, the decision was made to break into teams. Tasks were listed and delegated; calls were made. Sleep was at a premium, but team members grew increasingly motivated as the deadline approached. By 7:45 Saturday morning, men, women, and children were moving through food lines, piling their plates with hot barbecued chicken, scrambled eggs, burritos, bagels, donuts, and other donated goodies. Piles of neatly folded clothing were gratefully snapped up. By the time the food ran out at 11 a.m., 1,140 homeless people had been fed.

One of those participating later wrote about the experience, "When people tell me that they would like to do something but think it would be impossible, I think to myself, *Yeah, I used to think that way myself....*"[53]

The old adage, "There's strength in numbers" is still true. When people work together toward a common goal they can accomplish the impossible.

# Behind every successful man there's a lot of unsuccessful years.

■■■

*He lifted me out of the slimy pit,*
*out of the mud and mire;*
*he set my feet on a rock and*
*gave me a firm place to stand.*

Psalm 40:2

As a young man J.C. Penney ran a butcher shop. He was told that if he gave a fifth of Scotch to the head chef in a popular hotel, the business of that hotel would be his. Penney did this for some time. Then he felt convicted that what he was doing was wrong. He discontinued the gifts of liquor and sure enough, lost the hotel's business, causing him to go broke. God, however, had better things planned for him. In time, he began a merchandise business that grew into a nationwide enterprise.

Unsuccessful years alone don't create success. Remaining true to principles and doing the right thing — even when you seem to be failing — produces success eventually. A poem by an unknown writer says it well:

Who does God's work will get God's pay,
However long may seem the day,
However weary be the way;
Though powers and princes thunder "Nay,"
Who does God's work will get God's pay.

He does not pay as others pay,
In gold or land or raiment gay;
In goods that vanish and decay;
But God in wisdom knows a way,
And that is sure, let come what may,
Who does God's work will get God's pay.[54]

# Success generally depends upon knowing how long it takes to succeed.

■■■

*Perseverance must finish its work so that you may be mature and complete, not lacking anything.*

James 1:4

Catherine Ryan Hyde had written four unpublished novels and received more than five hundred rejection letters, when a call came from her agent that a publisher was eager to accept one of her novels. A check was mailed and Hyde's long wait for publication entered the home stretch. The novel she had written more than four years earlier, one rejected by more than a dozen publishers, had only a final round of revisions standing between it and a spring 1997 release.

That same month she also was named one of ten national finalists in the prestigious Raymond Carver Short Story Contest, the second time she had earned that honor. Hyde expects her latest novel, still under consideration by publishers, to go through several rejections and perhaps a rewrite. "All novels are rejected by someone, at some point," she has said. "You could have a novel with fifty separate rejection letters, but it could be accepted by someone else tomorrow. A rejection is always waiting to be turned into an acceptance."[55]

Those who expect overnight success are nearly always disappointed. Those who expect success laced with delays, errors, problems, and hard work are those who generally get what they expect — success included!

# No man will succeed unless he is ready to face and overcome difficulties and be prepared to assume responsibilities.

■■■

*If you want to build a tower, you first sit down and decide how much it will cost, to see if you have enough money to finish the job.*

Luke 14:28 NCV

As a young girl in the Great Depression, Debbie and her family lived with her grandparents because her father couldn't find work. She slept in a bed with four other relatives and survived by eating jackrabbits caught on the Texas plains. When she was seven, her family moved to California and at age sixteen, she won the Miss Burbank contest, which led to a part in a movie.

As an adult, her first marriage ended in a bitter divorce, so she raised her two children alone. Her second marriage to a millionaire shoe manufacturer ended when his financial gambles caused the failure of his business. He left her with millions of dollars in debt. Everything she owned was repossessed, including her home. Determined to pay back the debts and properly care for her family, she went on the road doing live theater. It took her more than ten years, working forty weeks a year, to pay back the debts of her ex-husband. But she did it.

Now out of debt and living in a home that is paid for, Debbie Reynolds has a satisfaction that only "doing the right thing" can produce.[56]

Successful people accept responsibility for their mistakes, and learn from their experiences. And most importantly, they never give up.

Many people have the ambition to succeed; they may even have a special aptitude for their job. And yet they do not move ahead. Why? Perhaps they think that since they can master the job, there is no need to master themselves.

■■■

*He that hath no rule over his own spirit is like a city that is broken down, and without walls.*

Proverbs 25:28 KJV

Long ago, a band of minstrels traveled from town to town performing music to make a living. They were not very financially successful. Times were hard and there was little money for common folk to spend on entertainment. Attendance was sparse.

One night, the troupe met to discuss their plight. One said, "I see no reason for singing tonight. It's starting to snow. Who will venture out on a night like this?" Another said, "I agree. Last night we performed for only a handful. Fewer will come tonight. Why not give back the price of their tickets and cancel." A third added, "It's hard to do one's best for so few."

Then an older man rose, and looking straight at the group as a whole, he said, "I know you are discouraged. I am too. It's not the fault of those who come that others do not. They should not be punished with less than the best we can give. We will go on and we will do our best."

Heartened by his words, the minstrels went on with their show. Even though the audience was small, they had never performed better. After the concert, the old man called the troupe together. "Listen to this," he said as he began to read a note he held in his hand: 'Thank you for a beautiful performance.'" The note was signed simply, "Your King."[57]

There are always at least two people who see what you do and how well you do it — you, and God.

# The recipe for successful achievement:

1. Enjoy your work.
2. Do your best.
3. Develop good working relationships.
4. Be open to opportunities.

■■■

*Blessed is the man who listens to me,*
*watching daily at my gates,*
*waiting at my doorposts.*
*For he who finds me finds life,*
*and obtains favor from the Lord.*

Proverbs 8:34,35 NASB

Marie Callender was making potato salad and cole slaw in a delicatessen in Los Angeles during World War II. Then one day her boss asked her to make pies for the lunch crowd. That was the start of a new career for her!

At first she baked her pies at home, dragging hundred-pound flour sacks into her kitchen. Then in 1948, she and her husband sold their car and bought a Quonset hut, an oven, and a refrigerator — her first commercial kitchen.

She baked pies that her husband delivered to restaurants in the area. She began by baking about ten pies a day. Two years later, she was baking more than two hundred pies a day. Sixteen years later, several thousand were coming out of the oven each day.

Marie and her husband opened their first pie shop in Orange County in 1964. They barely broke even that year. Over time her husband, and later her son guided the business to a soaring success. Other items were added to the menu, and by 1986, Ramada Inns, Inc. bought the family business — 115 restaurants at that time — from Marie and her son for $90 million.[58]

If a young mother with a rolling pin and sack of flour could give rise to an empire, think what other opportunities await those who will respond with hard work and a "better recipe."

A long time ago a noted specialist said that his secret of success as a physician was keeping the patient's head cool and his feet warm. And it is just now becoming generally known that a "hot head" and "cold feet" are enough to bring disaster to even a well man.

■■■

*He who is slow to anger is better than the mighty, and he who rules his spirit than he who takes a city.*

Proverbs 16:32 NKJV

For years, speed skater Dan Jansen didn't believe he could win a 1000-meter race. The 500 was his specialty. However, in the wake of his failures at the 1988 Olympics and the death of his sister, Jane, Jansen sought the help of a sports psychologist, Dr. Jim Loehr. One of the things that Loehr insisted that Jansen do was to write "I love the 1000," as often as possible. Jansen felt silly at first. But when he finally won a 1000-meter race, he wrote on the hotel stationery, "Maybe I really do love the 1000."

In the 1992 Olympics at Lillehammer, Jansen slipped during his 500-meter race, just enough of a falter to take him out of medal contention. "I love the 1000," became his personal mantra for the next three days — he put it on his training charts, in a bathroom drawer, on the refrigerator, on the bedroom mirror. Dr. Loehr had taught him, "You can go down, but make sure you come back up." Jansen was determined to do so. When the 1000-meter race began, he saw no reason to hold back. He felt both the courage and the calm to give it his all. He was thoroughly convinced, *I love the 1000*. He skated the best 1000-meter race of his life, and won the gold medal in a performance that inspired the world.[59]

Courage and calm are a winning combination in any arena!

No wind blows in favor of a ship without a destination.

■■■

*I press toward the goal for the prize of the upward call of God in Christ Jesus.*

Philippians 3:14 NKJV

It has been reported that when Christopher Columbus was nearing the American continent, he saw floating on the ocean swells an encouraging sign. Moving toward him in the water was a small tree branch. Its leaves were green — a significant sign that land could not be far away. At the time, the crews aboard Columbus' ships were greatly disheartened and on the verge of mutiny. The branch gave them a burst of enthusiasm, and not long after its discovery, the sailor at the topmast rang out the cry that thrilled all their hearts, "Land ahead! Land!"

What is amazing to most historians is that the crews of Columbus ever got far at all. It was not uncommon for seafaring ventures to the west of Europe to be abandoned early in a voyage. Those who set sail before Columbus were "explorers," who had little conviction that they might actually find something of value. What made Columbus' voyage different was that he truly believed — based upon evidence he had accumulated for years — that he could and would reach his destination. He was not simply an "explorer" of the waters. He was a man convinced he would find land on an opposite shore.[60]

Are you randomly "exploring" today, or do you have a specific destination in mind?

# If you don't like the road you're walking, start paving another one.

■■■

*Rise up; this matter is in your hands. We will support you, so take courage and do it.*

Ezra 10:4

Throughout the years she was raising her four children as a single mother, Marcia Meyer felt mostly powerless and inept when it came to money. She did keep faithful track of her earning and spending — it gave her a small sense of control in an otherwise chaotic life. Over time, Marcia grew determined to become financially independent. She was living with friends at the time, exchanging labor for room and board. She walked to a nearby motel and applied for a job as a maid. Several months later, she moved to Seattle to look for a job that paid more than minimum wage.

She began working for a temporary employment agency and started paying off several thousand dollars of debt. She charted her progress and was ruthless in evaluating each opportunity. She soon found a permanent position as an administrative assistant, but even then, she kept looking — reading want ads, talking to friends, keeping her ear to the ground. Then she volunteered at a medical conference and heard of a board that was looking for an executive director. Marcia was their choice. Her new annual salary was a figure that once would have been unthinkable to her.[61]

Is it time for you to start building a new highway?

Less is more
is true not only in
writing, but in life.

*Even a fool is thought wise*
*if he keeps silent, and discerning*
*if he holds his tongue.*
Proverbs 17:28

In *Living More With Less,* Doug Hostetter is quoted as saying, "The first thing I noticed when I arrived in Vietnam was the people really knew how to use bicycles. The streets of Saigon were crowded with them carrying whole families, literally four or five people. While Americans only ride a bicycle, Vietnamese also walked with it, using it as a wheelbarrow. They carried tables, chairs, bricks, wooden planks, bamboo, dozens of chickens or ducks, or even several pigs tucked into baskets.

> "I now live in New York and use a bicycle every day. I commute to work and save at least half an hour and one dollar daily. With a sturdy carrier for the back, I use it to take the wash to the laundry, pick up boxes at the post office, and carry friends. I keep a strap cut from an inner tube on the carrier to secure boxes....
>
> "A well-built bicycle is a work of art. It is one of the most efficient machines ever designed. It uses only human energy and is even more ecological than mass transit. It uses few resources in production or maintenance and doesn't pollute. It's quiet enough to let you think. In a congested city, bicycles actually save time over cars. A well-functioning one pays for itself in several months."[62]

Although a bicycle may be completely unrealistic for you, it is an excellent example of how less can actually be more.

# Success for the striver washes away the effort of striving.

■■■

*They that sow in tears shall reap in joy.*

Psalm 126:5 KJV

During World War II, England faced a need for more coal. As a result, Winston Churchill called labor leaders together to enlist their support. He presented a vision to them — the vision of a parade that he believed would one day be held in Piccadilly Circus.

First, the sailors who had kept the sea lanes open would come marching past. Then would come the soldiers who had held the lines in France and defeated Rommel in Africa. Then would come the pilots who had driven the Luftwaffe from the sky. Next, he envisioned a long line of sweat-stained, soot-streaked men in miner's caps would march by. Someone would cry from the crowd, "Where were you during the critical days of our struggle?" And the ten thousand men would proudly reply, "We were deep in the earth with our faces to the coal."

Inspired by Churchill's vision, the labor leaders rallied the support of their workers to increase output. When the workers realized that what they were doing was vital to winning the war, they were more than willing to make sacrifices and give extra effort. [63]

Mothers of newborns frequently say that they forgot the pain of their labor the moment they held their baby in their arms. Likewise, with all who have tasted success or have a strong vision for it. Success is its own greatest motivator. It wipes away the memory of the pain necessary to achieve it.

There is nothing like a fixed, steady aim, with an honorable purpose. It dignifies your nature, and insures your success.

■■■

*Therefore do not be foolish, but understand what the Lord's will is.*

Ephesians 5:17

For a boy named Sparky, school was nearly impossible. He failed every subject in the eighth grade and later, in high school, distinguished himself as the worst physics student in the school's history. He also flunked Latin, algebra, and English. He didn't find much success in sports and was awkward socially. He wasn't *disliked* by his peers; more accurately, nobody noticed him. He never had the nerve to ask a girl out on a date. He simply plodded along, knowing that he had the reputation of a loser.

One thing was important to Sparky, however. Drawing. He was proud of his own artwork even if no one else appreciated it. As a senior in high school, his cartoons were turned down by the editors of the school yearbook. In spite of this painful rejection, he believed he would one day become a professional artist. After graduation, he wrote to the Walt Disney Studios and sent samples of his work. He was rejected. So Sparky wrote his autobiography in cartoons, and soon, his portrayal of his own life was world famous.

Sparky, the nickname for Charles Schulz, had created the "Peanuts" comic strip. He *was* Charlie Brown.[64]

Every person has at least one talent. And if you develop it, that's all it takes.

If you have a good name...if you can face your God and say, "I have done my best," then you are a success.

■■■

*A good name is rather to be chosen than great riches, and loving favour rather than silver and gold.*

Proverbs 22:1 KJV

One summer day, Armstrong Williams was sent to the store by his father to buy wire and fencing for their farm. At 16, Armstrong liked nothing better than to be sent on errands in the family pickup, but this time his spirits were dampened. His father had told him to ask for credit. Williams feared what might happen. He had seen his black friends ask for credit and then stand with their head down, while a store owner questioned whether or not they were good for it. Nevertheless, there was no way to back out of the errand.

When he took his purchases to the register, he said cautiously, "I need to put this on credit." The middle-aged farmer standing next to him gave him an amused, cynical look. But the owner's face didn't change. "Sure," he said easily. "Your daddy is always good for it." Then he turned to the other man and said, "This here is one of James Williams' sons." The farmer nodded in a neighborly way, and young Armstrong was filled with pride. *James Williams' son*. Those three words had opened a door to an adult's respect. It was that day, Williams recalls, that he discovered a good name could carry with it a capital of good will, and that keeping the good name of his family was an important responsibility.[65]

Every person has the same opportunity to create a good reputation, regardless of their background.

# He that would have fruit must climb the tree.

■■■

*Put in the sickle,*
*for the harvest is ripe.*
Joel 3:13 NASB

The late Spencer Penrose, whose brother was a major political leader in Philadelphia in the late nineteenth century, was considered the "black sheep" of the family. He chose to live in the West, instead of the East. Fresh out of Harvard, he made his way to Colorado Springs in 1891. Not long after his move to Colorado, he wired his brother for $1500, so that he might go into a mining venture. His brother telegraphed him $150 instead — enough for train fare home — and warned him against the deal.

Years later, Spencer returned to Philadelphia and handed his brother $75,000 in gold coins — payment, he said, for his "investment" in his mining operation. His brother was stunned. He had qualms about accepting the money, however, and reminded his brother that he had advised against the venture and had only given him $150. "That," replied Spencer, "is why I'm giving you only $75,000. If you had sent me the full $1500 I requested, I would be giving you three-quarters of a million dollars."[66]

Nothing invested, nothing gained. Every harvest requires an initial seed. Be generous in your seed-sowing. Plant in good ground and you can anticipate a good return.

# The gent who wakes up and finds himself a success hasn't been asleep.

■■■

*Whatever your hand finds to do, do it with all your might.*

Ecclesiastes 9:10

On a December evening in 1995, the employees of Malden Mills in Lawrence, Massachusetts, thought their jobs had gone up in smoke. The mill had been destroyed by fire. But when morning came, the company leader, Aaron Feuerstein, told his 3,000-plus employees that he had decided to rebuild, immediately. Not only that, he intended to keep everyone on the payroll for thirty days. That decision cost him millions of dollars a week.

It was not the first time Feuerstein had disregarded the trends. When other textile mills in the area moved south to take advantage of lower taxes and cheaper labor, Feuerstein felt he had a responsibility to the people he employed, and stayed put.

When paychecks were handed out two days after the fire, each employee received a Christmas bonus and a note from the boss that read, "Do not despair. God bless each of you."

By January 2, the mill had reopened and within ninety days, 75 percent of the workers were back on the job. Experts had said it could never be done. The mill was able to fill 80 percent of its orders in spite of the fire. Feuerstein's investment in his employees had been returned to him in miracle-working effort and loyalty.[67]

When we give our best to others, we nearly always find that they give their best in return.

# The necessary ingredients for enjoying success:

1. Simple tastes
2. A certain degree of courage
3. Self-denial to a point
4. Love of work
5. A clear conscience

■■■

*We are confident that we have a good conscience, in all things desiring to live honorably.*

Hebrews 13:18 NKJV

One of the most influential and prominent people in the world is Pope John Paul II. Those who have known him through the years regard him as a man who has always had simple tastes, and lived an honorable life.

As a quarry worker in Poland in 1940, he endured bitterly cold temperatures dressed only in a sweat-soaked cap and blue cloth jacket and trousers. One day he arrived at work without his jacket — he had given it to someone he met on the road.

As a village cleric, he had a reputation as a "skinny priest in a threadbare cassock." He walked on an unpaved road to his first parish carrying all of his belongings in a battered briefcase. As a teacher of ethics at the Catholic University of Lublin, he often wore a black cassock frayed at the knees from the time he spent in prayer. As a cardinal at the Vatican, he owned practically nothing except his books, ecclesiastical robes, a few family mementos, skis, and hiking clothes.

Those who know him well have conjectured that it is because he has ties to so little in the way of family (most of whom died early in his life) or personal goods, that he is able to reach out so warmly to millions around the world who have very little to offer other than their faith.[68]

One's success is best enjoyed when greed and self-indulgence don't overshadow it.

# The most important single ingredient in the formula of success is knowing how to get along with people.

■■■

*In humility consider others better than yourselves. Each of you should look not only to your own interests, but also to the interests of others.*

Philippians 2:3,4

In *Bible Power for Successful Living,* Norman Vincent Peale tells of a man he calls Jeb. Early in his life, Jeb was so miserable that he attempted to kill himself by drinking poison. He succeeded only in burning his lips. When he recovered, his first thought was negative, *I can't even kill myself.* Then, a different thought took over, *Perhaps God has spared me for a purpose.* From that moment on, Jeb decided it was his purpose in life to make others happy. Everywhere he went for the next thirty years, Jeb left a trail of smiles and sunshine. He handed everyone he met a business card on which he had printed this message:

*The Way to Happiness*

Keep your heart free from hate, your mind free from worry.

Live simply; expect little; give much; fill your life with love; scatter sunshine.

Forget self.

Think of others, and do as you would be done by.

Try it for a week — you will be surprised.

Dr. Peale said Jeb was one of the happiest men that he had ever met.[69]

In your goals for success, have you included any goals that will help others find happiness?

Lasting success rarely comes to those who do not first decide to succeed.

*He knows enough to refuse evil and choose good.*

Isaiah 7:15 NASB

Charles Goodyear had no formal education. At the age of twenty-one, he went into partnership with his father in a hardware business that soon failed. It was the first of many losses. Failure and poverty characterized much of his life and more than once, he spent time in debtor's prison. His family frequently existed on the charity of neighbors. Six of his twelve children died in infancy. By the time he was forty, his health was very poor. He could not get around without the aid of crutches.

Most of Goodyear's troubles stemmed from his obsession with rubber. He had a fanatic determination to transform raw rubber into a useful material. To pursue his experiments, he sold his watch, the living room furniture, even the dishes off the table. Even when in jail, he experimented with rubber, trying to discover its unique properties and mold it to his satisfaction. Quite by accident, he stumbled upon the process of vulcanizing rubber when he dropped a piece of the material that had been treated with sulfur on a hot stove. He refined this process, which opened the development of an entire industry. While he might have amassed a fortune, his own bad judgment resulted in his dying in poverty.[70]

It takes more than effort and goals to gain *and keep* success. It also takes wisdom.

# We would accomplish many more things if we did not think of them as impossible.

■■■

*The things impossible with men are possible with God.*

Luke 18:27 NASB

John was a healthy, athletic, twenty-year-old who was gradually taking over the responsibilities of his family's dairy farm. Then one beautiful spring day while John was unloading fodder into the silage cutter, he put his foot into a large bunch of fodder that had stopped the conveyer belt, and before he knew it, his right leg and foot were caught in the machine. He managed to drag himself into the milk parlor of the dairy and call for an ambulance. While recovering in the hospital, he wished himself dead rather than handicapped. Then a middle-aged man in a wheelchair said to him, "Young man, shame on you whining away like that here. You should be thankful you are alive and healthy." He showed John that he had lost *both* of his legs. "Get well," he said, "then get out there and prove to the world that you can do as much with one leg as anyone else who has two legs."

John went back to the farm, and after a number of fittings for a mechanical leg and foot, he "regained" his life. He milks up to seventy cows a day and has taken over full management of the farm. In his leisure time, he swims, water-skis, snow skis. He is married and has three children.[71]

Does something in your life seem impossible? Think again!

# I have made mistakes, but I have never made the mistake of claiming that I never made one.

■■■

*Confess your faults one to another,*
*and pray one for another,*
*that ye may be healed.*

James 5:16 KJV

A young boy walked into a drugstore one day and asked to use the telephone. He dialed the operator and asked her to connect him with a certain number. When the party came on the line, the boy said, "Hello, Dr. Anderson...do you want to hire a boy to cut your grass and run errands for you?" After a pause he said, "Oh, you already have a boy? Are you completely satisfied with the job he's doing?" Another pause. "OK then, good-bye, Doctor."

As the boy thanked the druggist and prepared to leave, the druggist called to him. "Just a minute, son.... I couldn't help but overhear your conversation. If you are looking for work, I could sure use a boy like you."

"Thank you, sir," the boy replied, "but I have a job."

"You do?" the druggist responded. "But didn't I just hear you trying to get a job from Dr. Anderson?"

"No, sir," the boy said. "I'm the boy who is working for Dr. Anderson. I was just checking up on myself."[72]

One of the best ways to improve performance, avoid mistakes, and squelch pride — all at the same time — is to ask those with whom and for whom you work to give you suggestions on how you might do better, achieve more, and grow to the next level. When you check up on yourself, others don't feel it necessary to!

# Success is never final and failure never fatal. It's courage that counts.

■■■

*So we say with confidence, "The Lord is my helper; I will not be afraid. What can man do to me?"*

Hebrews 13:6

Sergio Zyman knows about failure. In 1984, Coca-Cola assigned him the challenge of reversing Coke's decline against Pepsi. Zyman's strategy was to replace Coke's formula with a sweeter "New Coke," and broadcast the change as widely as possible with a huge advertising campaign. His biggest mistake was in not keeping classic Coke on the market. Within seventy-nine days, the original formula was back on the shelves. New Coke was called the most disastrous new product launched since the Edsel. A year later, Zyman resigned from Coca-Cola.

Wounded and unwanted, Zyman didn't talk to anyone from the company for fourteen months, but he didn't burn any bridges. With the help of a partner, he started a consulting company, Core Strategy Group. With a computer, a phone, and a fax machine, he built a business advising clients as diverse as Miller Brewing and Microsoft. His message: think unconventionally, take risks. Eventually, even Coca-Cola sought his advice. "In my wildest dreams, I never thought the company would ask me back," Zyman admitted. Seven years after his failure, Zyman returned to Coca-Cola, his ego intact and his job expanded.[73]

Dolly Parton once said of her career, "I never stopped trying, and I never tried stopping."[74] Zyman would no doubt agree. Even your worst failure can be a building block toward success.

# Failure is the halfway mark on the road to success.

■■■

*For he has delivered me from all my troubles, and my eyes have looked in triumph on my foes.*

Psalm 54:7

Did you fall down the first time you tried to walk? Most likely. Did you feel as if you were drowning the first time you ventured into deep water? Probably. Did you hit the ball the first time you swung a bat? Probably not.

R. H. Macy failed seven times before his store in New York became popular.

English novelist John Creasey received 753 rejection slips prior to publishing 564 books.

Babe Ruth struck out 1,330 times, although he is best known for hitting 714 home runs.[75]

Michael Jordan didn't make the cut for his high school basketball team when he was a sophomore. He cried over his failure, but then tried harder. The next year he made the team, and never looked back.[76]

One salesman noted that he made one sale for about every ten "cold calls" he made. Each sale averaged about $1,000. Rather than be discouraged, then, when he was turned down, he'd simply say, "Well, I just made $100." He saw himself as one-tenth *closer* to a commission.

Don't expect *never* to fail. Expect occasional failure, learn from it, and move a lesson closer to your goal.

# Failure is often that early morning hour of darkness which precedes the dawning of the day of success.

■■■

*In the world ye shall have tribulation: but be of good cheer; I have overcome the world.*

John 16:33 KJV

After his butcher shop in Brooklyn had been robbed at gunpoint four times in one month, William Levine began to think his life might be in danger! He searched for and bought a bulletproof vest in 1980, shortly after they were invented and made available to the public.

Other proprietors in the area heard of Levine's purchase and one by one, came to him asking where they might also purchase such a vest. Levine began taking orders for them as a sideline.

Before long, Levine realized that there was more to be made in the bulletproof vest business than at his butcher shop. He became the full-time president of Body Armor, International. By the late 1980s, his company had forty sales representatives across the nation, and was selling five hundred to six hundred vests a month.[77]

We've all heard the phrase, "If life throws you lemons, make lemonade." Levine certainly did.

Stumbling and falling does not make you a failure. Failure is when you stay on the floor after you've fallen. Success comes in finding something while you're on the floor to pick up and carry away with you.

# I couldn't wait for success...so I went ahead without it.

■■■

*So David triumphed over the Philistine with a sling and a stone; without a sword in his hand he struck down the Philistine and killed him.*

1 Samuel 17:50

Are you waiting for perfect conditions before you set out to pursue your dreams? This poem by Edward Rowland Sill challenges that mindset.

*Opportunity*

This I beheld, or dreamed it in a dream:
There spread a cloud of dust along a plain;
And underneath the cloud, or in it, raged
A furious battle, and men yelled, and swords
Shocked upon swords and shields. A prince's banner
Wavered, then staggered backward, hemmed by foes.
A craven hung along the battle's edge
And thought, "Had I a sword of keener steel —
That blue blade that the king's son bears — but this
Blunt thing — !" He snapt and flung it from his hand,
And lowering, crept away and left the field.
Then came the king's son, wounded, sore bestead,
And weaponless, and saw the broken sword,
Hilt-buried in the dry and trodden sand,
And ran and snatched it, and with battle-shout
Lifted afresh, he hewed his enemy down,
And saved a great cause that heroic day.[78]

Don't overlook the potential of what you already hold in your hand.

# Success requires the vision to see, the faith to believe, and the courage to do.

■■■

*Be on your guard; stand firm in the faith; be men of courage; be strong.*

1 Corinthians 16:13

In 1990, Bill and Gina Ellis were living a comfortable life in Los Angeles. Then just before Christmas, Bill was laid off from his job. To distract themselves from the loss during the holiday season, they reviewed sketches of a sofa Gina had seen in Spain. The style lent itself to washable slipcovers that could be changed with the seasons. They made slight variations in the design and had the sofa custom-built. Their friends raved.

Bill took a long hard look at drawings he had of other pieces of furniture. He said impulsively, "We could *sell* these." Gina agreed, and within a week they had launched Quatrine Washable Furniture. Using equity from their house, they leased a small shop and paid a craftsman to construct their first five sofas and chairs. Customers loved their furniture, but felt it was too expensive.

Then about three months after they started their venture, a woman came into their shop, selected several pieces of furniture, and wrote a check for $14,000. They then used some of the money to create a line of more reasonably priced furniture. By summer, the new pieces were ready. They moved their business to Detroit and eventually opened branches in Dallas, Chicago, and Denver. By 1996, their sales totaled more than $5 million a year.[79]

Reward cannot be separated from vision, risk, and courage.

# There are no shortcuts to any place worth going.

■■■

*The gate is small and the road is narrow that leads to true life.*

Matthew 7:14 NCV

These days, we take our interstate highway system for granted. Our county road system in the United States is better than that found in many nations of the world. What we generally forget is that not more than two hundred years ago, much of America was still a wild and uncharted territory. For the most part, there were no roads, or even trails.

In 1830, not even a trail to follow the hundred miles between Iowa City, Iowa, and Dubuque, the state capital. If a person needed to make that journey in those days, he had to trek straight across an untracked, rugged landscape.

A farmer who had settled in Iowa City decided that something needed to be done about it. He took matters into his own hands. He hitched a team of oxen to a plow and started across the wilderness making a furrow as he went. It took him months to complete it. He had barely finished before the people of that region began to travel along the furrow in both directions, using it as a guide. As a result, the ground on either side of it was soon beaten into a highway.[80]

If you see a trail that needs to be beaten, start walking. Others will soon join you and your trail may become a highway.

# Don't wait for your ship to come in; swim out to it.

■■■

*I am the Lord, who opened a way through the waters, making a path right through the sea.*

Isaiah 43:16 TLB

Don played the tambourine in junior high, and that seemed about the extent of his musical ability — at least in the opinion of his peers. They recall that he couldn't carry a tune in a bucket. However, Don considered himself to be a musician.

When his friends graduated and went on to college, Don packed his things and moved to Nashville. He bought a used car and slept in it, took a job working nights so he could visit record companies during the day, and learned to play the guitar. For years, he practiced, wrote songs, and knocked on doors, with virtually no breaks. Then one day, his old friends heard a song on the radio. It was a good song. A good singer, who was rising on the country charts. It was Don Schlitz singing a song he had written and recorded.

A short time later, Kenny Rogers recorded one of Don's songs. "The Gambler" became the title song for one of the best-selling country-music albums of the 80s. Don has since written twenty-three number-one hits.[81]

Don didn't wait for fame and fortune to come to him. He went in search of them.

There's an old saying among business planners that can apply to virtually every area of your life: Plan your work, then work your plan. Go for your goals. Don't expect them to arrive on your doorstep in a neatly packaged bundle.

Every man should make up his mind that if he expects to succeed, he must give an honest return for the other man's dollar.

■■■

*But as for me, I walk in my integrity.*

Psalm 26:11 NRSV

As a young man, William learned an important lesson from his father, who worked in a shop that made dies. His dad explained, "That's a fancy word for molds used to manufacture plastic dishes like this cup. Make 'em right, and they last a lifetime." He then held up a cup and asked William, "What do you think would happen if I dropped it?" William replied, "It would smash." His father dropped the cup and instead of breaking, it bounced several times but didn't even crack. His father said proudly, "One good man can make a die that can make tens of thousands of cups."

William's father introduced him to the die-maker squinting to read a micrometer, the journeyman transforming a piece of rough-cut steel into a mold, and the pressman stamping out a finished product. Then he said, "Know what I see? I see that it's not good enough." His father switched on a powerful magnifying lamp and let his son see what he saw — tiny pit marks in the mold that compromised the mold's integrity. "If we had used that die for a week, we'd have multiplied our errors a thousand-fold," he explained. "Quality is what satisfies the customer *and* the producer."[82]

True satisfaction comes not in just getting a job done, but in getting it done *right.*

# Character is the real foundation of all worthwhile success.

■■■

*Walk in the way of goodness, and keep to the paths of righteousness. For the upright will dwell in the land.*

Proverbs 2:20,21 NKJV

The son of an English skipper was confirmed one Palm Sunday morning. Later that day, the skipper sat with his son in his cabin. He was anxious to do what he could to reinforce the meaning of the service that his son had experienced that morning. He said to the young man, "Son, light this candle, go out on the deck, and return to the cabin with the candle burning."

"But Father," the boy protested, "if I go on the deck, the wind will surely blow it out."

"Go," the father said, "do it." So the son went. With much shielding and maneuvering, he managed to keep the flame burning, and he returned the candle to his father with a sense of relief and accomplishment. His father then said to him, "Son, you were confirmed today. Your faith is still small and frail. You are growing up and are about to enter the big, tempting world that will do its best to snuff out the flame of your faith...unless you properly shield it." It was a vivid lesson the boy never forgot.[83]

Character — the most vital ingredient of success — isn't something that just "happens." It must be thoughtfully nurtured, consistently cultivated, and carefully guarded.

# It takes twenty years to make an overnight success.

■■■

*Diligent hands will rule,*
*but laziness ends in slave labor.*

Proverbs 12:24

Twenty years ago, a microbiologist from the University of Illinois had a new theory concerning life. Until Carl Woese stated his theory, it was accepted as absolute fact that the "tree of life" had two branches: bacteria and eukarya, which is made up of all advanced plants and animals, including human beings. After much research, however, Woese announced his belief that there was a third branch.

The scientific community scoffed. Then in 1995, scientist J. Craig Venter began to examine Woese's theory.

Venter worked on specimens that a group of scientists had plucked from a spot three kilometers beneath the surface of the Pacific Ocean in 1982. One was a methane-producing organism, a microbe never before seen. Venter and other researchers began working on a blueprint of the microbe's genes. In 1996, the research was completed, and it was clear to all that this microbe represented a third branch of life: archaea.

It took twenty years, but Woese had finally been vindicated. Those who had scoffed were now forced to admit he had been right all along. Woese no doubt took a great deal of satisfaction from the statement made by a California microbiologist, Norman R. Pace, who said simply, "It's time to rewrite the textbooks."[84,85]

Diligence applied to what is right *will* result in success.

# To climb steep hills requires slow pace at first.

■■■

*Though your beginning was small, yet your latter end would greatly increase.*

Job 8:7 AMP

Scott McGregor worked for a company that rented cellular phones to business travelers. The phones were not designed, however, to produce itemized bills and some corporations refused to reimburse their employees without one. Each phone needed a computer chip to keep a billing record of each call.

McGregor quit his job and began to pursue the idea full-time. He felt sure it was a winner. After two years of effort, however, he had met with very little success and faced being evicted from his home. At the eleventh hour, he found an investor willing to help him turn his idea into a reality.

McGregor used part of the money to hire a consulting engineer, but after several months the engineer said the system McGregor wanted was impossible. He already had an appointment to demonstrate a prototype to BellSouth, so he called his twenty-two-year-old son, Greg, who was a computer science major. Greg began working up to eighteen hours a day to create the automated circuit that would defy the experts. He and his Dad flew to Atlanta to meet with BellSouth and his solution worked.

Today, the McGregor family firm, Telemac Cellular Corporation, is an industry leader worth millions of dollars.[86]

A slow start diligently pursued can result in a big finish.

# Always aim for achievement and forget about success.

■■■

*So we make it our goal to please him.*

2 Corinthians 5:9

Lord of all pots and pans and things,
Since I've no time to be
A saint by doing lovely things,
Or watching late with Thee,
Or dreaming in the dawnlight,
Or storming heaven's gates,
Make me a saint by getting meals,
And washing up the plates.

Although I have Martha's hands,
I have a Mary's mind;
And when I black the boots and shoes,
Thy sandals, Lord, I find.
I think of how they trod the earth,
Each time I scrub the floor.
Accept this meditation, Lord,
I haven't time for more.

Warm all the kitchen with Thy love,
And light it with Thy peace;
Forgive me all my worrying,
And make all grumbling cease.
Thou who didst love to give men food,
In a room or by the sea,
Accept this service that I do —
I do it unto Thee.[87]

—Unknown

# To follow, without halt, one aim: There's the secret of success.

■■■

*But Jesus told him, "Anyone who lets himself be distracted from the work I plan for him is not fit for the Kingdom of God."*

Luke 9:62 TLB

On July 23, 1989, Greg LeMond had one goal: to get to Paris as fast as he possibly could. He was about to begin the final leg of the Tour de France, the world's most famous bicycle race. He was starting the day, however, fifty seconds behind the leader, Larent Fignon of France. Furthermore, the final leg of the race was only about fifteen miles, a distance that all the experts said was too short for LeMond to have a chance of catching Fignon. But the experts couldn't see into the heart and mind of Greg LeMond.

LeMond knew about fortitude. On a hunting trip in April of 1987, he was accidentally shot by his brother-in-law. Sixty shotgun pellets ripped through his back and side. It was the worst pain he had ever known, but miraculously he survived. Thirty of the pellets remained in his body, two of those in his heart. The road back to championship racing had been brutal and punishing. At one point he nearly quit. That same year, he had an emergency appendectomy and the year later, a tendon injury that required surgery. But now LeMond was focused. Riding faster than anyone could believe, he crossed the finish line first and won the Tour de France by scarcely the length of a bicycle.[88]

The path to success is never smooth. The key is to stay focused on your goal, pick up your feet, and get going.

# The world is not interested in the storms you encountered, but did you bring in the ship?

■■■

*[Jesus] got up, rebuked the wind and said to the waves, "Quiet! Be still!" Then the wind died down and it was completely calm.*
*He who believes in Me, the works that I do shall he do also.*

Mark 4:39 NIV & John 14:12 NASB

Debora Dempsey, captain of the transport ship *Lyra,* was glad to be at home. The storm that raged off Cape Fear on January 26, 1993, was a sailor's nightmare. She thought she had seen her 634-ton ship for the last time the day it left Chesapeake Bay on its way to a buyer in New Orleans. Then Dempsey received a call. Northeast of Cape Fear, the *Lyra* had broken loose from its towline. The crewless ship — with 387,000 gallons of oil on board to run its engines — was being pushed toward land by the strong winds. An ecological disaster was in the making, not to mention the loss of the $22 million vessel. Dempsey and four volunteer crew members were called upon to save the ship and avert disaster.

Lowered from a helicopter onto the pitching deck, they immediately began to lower the two 5-1/2-ton anchors. After they got the first anchor safely down, the generator failed. Without the aid of a power winch, using only flashlights, they finally got the second anchor down, stopping the ship's deadly drift. It was a dangerous mission, accomplished only by a strong team effort. Dempsey received the Admiralty of the Ocean Sea award, a high honor, for her leadership and courage.[89]

Effort may be self-rewarding, but it is accomplishment of a goal that brings recognition. Often the best way to *complete* the task is teamwork.

# The measure of success is not whether you have a tough problem to deal with, but whether it's the same problem you had last year.

■■■

*But the God of all grace, who hath called us unto his eternal glory by Christ Jesus, after that ye have suffered a while, make you perfect, stablish, strengthen, settle you.*

1 Peter 5:10 KJV

For years, farmers in southern Alabama had one mainstay crop: cotton. They plowed as much ground as they could each year to plant their big cash crop, and year after year, they lived by their cotton production. Then one year, the dreaded boll weevil devastated the entire area's crops. Optimistic that the tragedy was an isolated event, the farmers mortgaged their homes and planted cotton again the next year, hoping for a big harvest to help them recoup their losses. But once again, the insect destroyed the crop, and as a result, most of the farmers were wiped out.

The few farmers who were able to survive two years of boll weevil infestation decided to do something they had never done before the third year — plant peanuts. The peanuts proved to be resistant to insects and the market was strong. Most of those who planted peanuts were able to reap enough profit that third year to pay off all their debts. They chose to plant peanuts from that point on, and they greatly prospered.

In the following years, the farmers actually erected a monument to their old enemy, the boll weevil. They concluded that if it hadn't been for the boll weevil, they never would have discovered peanuts.[90]

If a problem forces you to take a detour, don't be discouraged. You may find it is a better road!

# The strength of a man consists in finding out the way God is going, and going that way.

■■■

*My soul shall be joyful in the Lord;
it shall rejoice in His salvation.*

Psalm 35:9 NKJV

When Orv Krieger, a hotel broker, received a call about a property for sale in Spokane, Washington, he decided to take the plunge and buy it himself rather than list it for sale. He knew the 140-unit Holiday Inn — minutes from the airport and located on thirteen acres of fir-covered hillside overlooking the city — was a prime property.

Krieger quickly discovered that the Inn's restaurant was the big money-maker. The bar grossed an average of $10,000 a month. But Krieger's Christian principles were incompatible with running a business subsidized by alcohol sales. The motel manager argued that if guests couldn't get a drink at the Inn, they'd be off to other hotels in a flash. He had convincing statistics for his argument, but Krieger closed the bar anyway. The manager resigned.

Krieger remodeled the hotel lobby, and replaced the bar area with a cozy coffee shop filled with greenery. In the first five years of business, food sales went up 20 percent and bookings were up 30 percent. Profits might not have been what they *could* have, but they were substantial enough to satisfy Krieger. He has said, "Beliefs aren't worth much if a fella's not ready to live by them."[91]

Always keep in mind that God holds the keys to all locked doors. Find out which door He desires to open for you and then walk through it.

# Four steps to achievement: plan purposefully, prepare prayerfully, proceed positively, pursue persistently.

■■■

*Now all the work of Solomon was well-ordered from the day of the foundation of the house of the Lord until it was finished. So the house of the Lord was completed.*

2 Chronicles 8:16 NKJV

No one is born an achiever. Achievement comes through developing competency and working hard. Jack Nicklaus knows this well. He has said, "I don't think talent is as important as the work and the dedication necessary to become competent." Nicklaus readily admits that there are hundreds of talented golfers who never made it on the pro circuit. "You see guys," he says, "and you say, 'Gosh, how did this guy not make it?' And then it's pretty easy to figure out why he didn't. He had a lot of talent, but didn't have much dedication, wasn't organized, didn't know how to learn, didn't know how to comprehend what he was doing, didn't try to learn to get better.... I think the big thing about doing anything is striving to improve every day. I'm learning new shots every day. I worked on a couple of new shots yesterday — ones I didn't have in my game. I spent about two hours working on a specific shot yesterday that I didn't have. I got it today."

Nicklaus now competes on the senior circuit. He says, "I'm not as talented as I was ten or fifteen years ago, 'cause I just don't have the physical ability. That's why I have to compete in another way. I have to compete with my mind — compete with a larger variety of shots."[92]

Basic to all plans, preparations, and persistence should be the willingness to work hard and learn more.

# The secret of all victory lies in the organization of the non-obvious.

■■■

*But God hath chosen the foolish things of the world to confound the wise; and God hath chosen the weak things of the world to confound the things which are mighty.*

1 Corinthians 1:27 KJV

Today if you tried to cook something by "handfuls" and "heaping spoonfuls," the odds of producing a tasty dish would definitely be against you. Especially if you were using someone else's recipe and you had never seen the dish prepared. Yet, for countless generations, this is precisely how people cooked. And then Fannie Farmer brought precision into the kitchen, earning herself the nickname, "The Mother of Level Measurements."

Farmer herself was a poor cook in her youth. After suffering and recovering from a stroke as a teenager, she went to work as a "mother's helper" to aid her father's failing printing business. While cooking for the family one day, the daughter in the family asked her whether it wouldn't be more consistent to use two level spoonfuls instead of one heaping one. Farmer agreed!

Then, at the age of thirty, she enrolled in the Boston Cooking School and after two years of training, became the assistant principal. Five years later, she was put in charge of the school and soon after published *The Boston Cooking-School Cookbook*. Unlike any cookbook ever published, hers was precise, every recipe tested repeatedly. Her book is still in print, updated through at least twelve editions.[93]

There is almost always a way to simplify a task, making it more efficient and consistent. People who are able to do this are usually very successful at whatever they choose to do.

# Success in life comes not from holding a good hand, but in playing a poor hand well.

■■■

*To him who overcomes,*
*I will grant to eat of the tree of life.*

Revelation 2:7 NASB

With a Ph.D. in organic chemistry and a good teaching job at an Ivy League medical school, John Castelli felt like a winner. He had a dependable income, prestige in his neighborhood, and his father's undying admiration.

For ten years, Castelli did his job well and enjoyed a comfortable routine. And then, the man at the university who sponsored his research, left. His next annual grant proposal was turned down. Castelli was out of a position.

He became excruciatingly familiar with the local unemployment office and job application forms. Then one day a neighbor asked Castelli if he knew someone who could paint the exterior of her house. As a carpenter's son, Castelli had firsthand experience with home-improvement projects. He also was deeply in debt, so he swallowed his pride and offered to do the job himself.

Other neighbors quickly learned of Castelli's talents, and before long, he had as many jobs as he could handle. Being a handyman didn't have the same "prestige" as being a university professor, but it was honorable work and Castelli was soon earning as much as he had as a teacher.

What at first appeared to be a "poor hand" — a step backward — became a chance for a different kind of life.[94]

When God closes a door, He opens a window elsewhere. We just have to be willing to climb through it.

# The talent of success is nothing more than doing what you can do well; and doing well whatever you do, without a thought of fame.

■■■

*But remember the Lord your God, for it is he who gives you power to get wealth, so that he may confirm his covenant that he swore to your ancestors.*

Deuteronomy 8:18 NRSV

During the Russian Civil War, Alexander M. Poniatoff was a pilot in the czar's military. Later he worked as an engineer in China, before finally coming to the United States in 1927. In 1944, he founded Ampex, a company he named using his initials plus "ex" for excellence. Under his leadership, Charles Ginsburg and Ray M. Dolby developed the videotape recorder.

Ampex premiered its machine at a national broadcasting industry convention in April 1956, beating out RCA, which was also working on the invention. The demand for VTRs exceeded all Poniatoff's expectations and within a dozen years the value of his company more than doubled, to $220 million. The machine was used for one of the foremost media events of the era, the famous Nixon-Khrushchev "kitchen debate" that was held at the Ampex booth of an American trade expo in Moscow in July 1959.

By the time Poniatoff died in 1980, the company he founded earned half a billion dollars a year. His engineers licensed Ampex's tape technology to a rising Japanese company, Sony, which introduced the videocassette recorder.[95]

Poniatoff is not a household name, but today you will find the product his company pioneered in almost every American home. Poniatoff didn't seek fame, only to invent.

A winner is someone who recognizes his God-given talents, works his tail off to develop them into skills, and uses these skills to accomplish his goals.

■■■

*The man who had received the five talents brought the other five. "Master," he said, "you entrusted me with five talents. See, I have gained five more."*

Matthew 25:20

I have no voice for singing,
I cannot make a speech,
I have no gift for music,
I know I cannot teach.

I am no good at leading,
I cannot "organize,"
And anything I write
Would never win a prize.

But at roll call in meetings
I always answer, "Here."
When others are performing
I lend a listening ear.

After the program's over,
I praise its every part.
My words are not to flatter,
I mean them from my heart.

It seems my only talent
Is neither big nor rare,
Just to listen and encourage
And to fill a vacant chair.

But all the gifted people
Could not so brightly shine,
Were it not for those who use
A talent such as mine![96]

—Alice Barbour Bennett

There is no limit
to the good
a man can do
if he doesn't care
who gets the credit.

■■■

*"My food," said Jesus,*
*"is to do the will of him who sent me*
*and to finish his work."*

John 4:34

The young people at Shively Christian Church were fiercely competitive with their neighboring church, Shively Baptist, especially in softball. They were also serious about attending the summer Bible camp led by their youth pastor, Dave Stone. After teaching a Bible lesson about Jesus washing His disciples' feet, Pastor Stone divided the kids into groups and challenged them to find a practical way to serve others. "I want you to be Jesus in the city for the next two hours," he said. At the end of the two hours, the kids met to report on what they had done.

One group had done yard work for an elderly man. Other groups had taken ice cream treats to several widows, visited a church member in the hospital, and sung Christmas carols at a nursing home, even though it was August.

The final group's report made everyone groan. They had gone to the Shively Baptist pastor and asked him to recommend someone who needed help. He sent them to an elderly woman who needed yard work done. She had thanked them for their hard work saying, "You kids at Shively Baptist are always coming to my rescue."

Pastor Stone interrupted, "I hope you set her straight and told her you were from Shively *Christian.*" "No," the kids said, "we really didn't think it mattered."[97]

# There is no substitute for hard work.

■■■

*He who cultivates his land will have plenty of bread, but he who follows worthless people and pursuits will have poverty enough.*

Proverbs 28:19 AMP

Arnold Schwarzenegger was a skinny teenager living in Austria when, in spite of his parents' doubts, he threw himself into weightlifting. He went to the local gym three times a week, and each evening he worked out at home for several hours. Today the champion bodybuilder, turned actor, is the biggest box-office draw in the history of movies — to a great extent because of his physique.

When Condoleezza Rice was in high school, she was told that her test scores showed she probably wouldn't do well in college. She didn't take that to heart. Instead, she modeled herself after her grandfathers — one of whom had worked three jobs to support his family, and the other who had completed college in 1920. She threw herself into her studies with such concentrated energy that she entered the University of Denver at age 15, and graduated Phi Beta Kappa at 19. At age 41, Rice became the youngest provost in the history of Stanford University, the first woman and the first African-American to fill that prestigious post.

Psychologist John E. Anderson, who has worked with athletes, executives, artists, and young people, has said, "I've learned that those who rise to the headiest heights in any field aren't necessarily the ones with the greatest natural talent. They're the diligent few who put in the hours. They work hard. And then they work harder."[98]

If you succeed
in all you do,
it's a sure sign
you're not
reaching
high enough.

■■■

*Seek those things which are above.*

Colossians 3:1 NKJV

One day during the early 1960s, the University of Florida football team was in a practice session. They were running wind sprints for conditioning. One of the large linemen, Jack Katz, had proven himself to be the fastest lineman on the team.

Katz went to Coach Ray Graves and asked if he might be allowed to run sprints with the faster and smaller backfield players. Permission was granted.

For the next several days, Katz managed to finish last in every race with the backfield runners. Nobody was surprised. The coach went to Katz to ask if he wouldn't rather go back to winning against the other linemen, rather than lose every race against the backs.

Katz responded, "I'm not out here to outrun the linemen. I already know I can do that. I'm here to learn how to run faster; and if you've noticed, I'm losing by a little less every day."

Indeed, a lineman's job is not only to break through and scatter the line on the other team, but also to tackle its backfield players. Katz was preparing himself for his ultimate goal: real-game tackles.[99]

When you master one level, go on to the next. It is the only way to keep growing and developing your skills!

# Those who aim low usually hit their targets.

■■■

*For as he thinketh in his heart, so is he.*

Proverbs 23:7 KJV

A frustrated young man once consulted a man whom he perceived to be highly successful. "Success completely eludes me. I want to get somewhere," he said.

"That's great!" the successful man replied. "And exactly where do you want to get?"

His reply was inconclusive. "Well, I don't know for sure; never figured that one out. But I'm not happy with the way things are. I think I'm entitled to a better break. I want to get somewhere."

The successful man probed, "What can you do best? What particular skills do you have? What do you think you're cut out for?" The young man pondered the question and then said, "I don't believe I have any particular skills. I've thought about it."

The successful man tried a third time, "What would you *like* to do if you could have any job you wanted?" The answer was vague, "I can't really tell you. I just don't know what I like best."

The successful man advised, "Fix on a goal. Sharpen and clarify it. Hold it in your mind until it sinks in. Then, you can begin to move toward your goal, not to a vague 'somewhere,' but to a specific destination."[100]

If you don't know where you want to go, how will you ever know when you have arrived?

Do in life what you would do even if no one paid you for it — do what you are passionate about. Soon men will pay almost anything for your services.

■■■

*Do you see a man skilled in his work?*
*He will serve before kings;*
*he will not serve before obscure men.*

Proverbs 22:29

"Today" show anchor Katie Couric once advised a group of people just starting out on their careers, "Believe in yourself and do something you love. My job gives me access to some of the most successful people in the world. I've found one common denominator among them. They all love their jobs. Dictionary synonyms for work include 'toil,' 'drudgery,' and 'travail.' Those should be antonyms, not synonyms. If you love what you're doing, success will follow. Grabbing the brass ring isn't fulfilling if you don't enjoy the merry-go-round."[101]

Every job has a certain degree of drudgery. That's life. A well-known Broadway stage designer once remarked, "I hate the business side of my job — the worrying about payroll and paying vendors. I like the pitching of ideas and the creative give-and-take with directors and producers. But I love the design work. I'd be sketching and painting even if nobody wanted to buy my ideas. And since I spend the great bulk of my time designing, I love my job. I wouldn't dream of doing anything else."

Keep in perspective what it is that drew you to your line of work in the first place. Rekindle that aspect of your work that you love the most. Therein lies your success.

# The successful person is the individual who forms the habit of doing what the failing person doesn't like to do.

■■■

*Go watch the ants, you lazy person.*
*Watch what they do and be wise.*

Proverbs 6:6 NCV

Every baby born in a U.S. hospital is given an "Apgar score" within sixty seconds after birth — even before the baby is wrapped in a blanket and handed to its mother. This quick evaluation of the baby's heart rate, breathing, muscle tone, reflexes, and skin color provides doctors with the first evidence of whether the newborn needs special help.

This procedure did not become a systematic part of delivery room practice until Dr. Virginia Apgar developed the scoring system in 1952. One of the few female medical students at Columbia University in the early 1930s, Apgar was studying to be a surgeon, but switched to anesthesiology. It was by working as the anesthesiologist during thousands of deliveries that she realized doctors and nurses gave more immediate attention to the mother than to her newborn baby. "I kept wondering," she has said, "who was really responsible for the newborn. Birth is the most hazardous time of life."[102]

Before Apgar's test was developed, delivery doctors and nurses hadn't really paid much attention to the baby, they knew what to do for the mother. Her test has saved the lives of thousands of infants, by teaching doctors and nurses what to look for to ensure an infant is healthy. She simply noticed that something, or someone, was being overlooked.

# You have to experience failure in order to understand success.

■■■

*If you do what the Lord wants, he will make certain each step you take is sure. The Lord will hold your hand, and if you stumble, you still won't fall.*

Psalm 37:23,24 CEV

Since finishing his prison term for the part he played in the Watergate scandal, Charles Colson has been doing the opposite of what most people expected of him: rather than avoid prisons, he has been the primary force behind Prison Fellowship, a ministry to prisoners.

One Easter Sunday, during a visit to a Delaware prison, Colson attended a breakfast organized by Christian inmates. A man serving a life sentence read a poem he'd written to thank Colson for his work. After breakfast, outside the prison chapel, he saw inmates carrying signs that read, "COME TO THE CHAPEL" and "JESUS SETS THE PRISONERS FREE!" — a bold move in any prison.

Colson thought about the word "success." Before the Watergate scandal, he was an American success story. From scholarships to courtroom victories, to serving as special counsel to the President, he was regarded as a very successful man. But that day in Delaware, Colson realized that he was finally seeing success from God's point of view. He has written, "The real legacy of my life was my biggest failure, that I was an ex-convict. Only when I lost everything I thought made Chuck Colson a great guy had I found the true self God intended me to be.... My greatest humiliation — being sent to prison — was the beginning of God's greatest use of my life."[103]

# A wise man will make more opportunity than he finds.

■■■

*A man's gift maketh room for him, and bringeth him before great men.*

Proverbs 18:16 KJV

Jose's father died suddenly while he was a student on scholarship at Columbia University. In order to help out with the family business, Jose took a leave of absence from Columbia. Through long hours of work Jose Aguiar, Jr., saved his father's dry cleaning business, but before he knew it, three years had slipped by. He had lost his college scholarship. When his former classmates invited him to their graduation parties, he was too depressed to attend.

Like other dry cleaners, Aguiar faced increasing environmental regulation, and competition from "drop-store" chains served by central cleaning plants. When he approached franchise promoters, he was rebuffed. They weren't interested in inner cities. Aguiar thought, *Thousands of people in the Bronx carry their cleaning into Manhattan on their way to work. An enormous opportunity is being overlooked.* He became excited about the idea of starting his own franchise. In 1992, he launched Kleener King, a chain that had 22 stores by 1996, all managed by residents of the inner-city neighborhoods they serve.

Recently, Aguiar contacted Columbia University about going back part-time to earn a degree. Instead, he was asked to lecture their business students![104]

One of the greatest opportunities any person has is to turn a problem into a solution.

A failure is a man who has blundered, but is not able to cash in on the experience.

■■■

*Correct those with understanding, and they will gain knowledge.*

Proverbs 19:25 NCV

After teaching a seminar about Jesus' unconditional love, Ruth Carter Stapleton invited people to meet with her for prayer. A man who had attended every session came forward. He told her that more than thirty years ago, he had gone by boat to another country to work at a resort hotel. Upon arrival, he found that his only pay for scrubbing floors, lighting the furnace, and doing other chores would be room and board. Disillusioned, he decided to take the next boat home.

The following morning, he tried to light the furnace as he had been shown, but only some of the burners ignited. Since they seemed to be burning well, he turned them up, went to his room, packed his suitcase, and left the hotel. As he walked toward the dock, he heard an explosion. Looking back, he saw the hotel engulfed in flames. He ran for the boat, and had been running ever since. "Do you think Christ can forgive me?" he asked. Stapleton assured him that Jesus would indeed forgive his misdeed. The man began to sob, and then said, "It's gone." He explained that since the day of the explosion he had had a lump in his throat, and now it was gone, along with his guilt and shame.[105]

The greatest "cashing in" you can ever do for a sin is to turn it over to God and receive His forgiveness.

# More people talk themselves into failure than talk themselves into success.

■■■

*Your words now reflect your fate then: either you will be justified by them or you will be condemned.*

Matthew 12:37 TLB

In an article on constructive thinking, Bibi Wein describes how one woman interpreted her day:

"These are some things that happened to Ellen on a typical day: Her supervisor unexpectedly agreed to a project she'd proposed. Her daughter came home with an A on a math test. Her father, who was recently hospitalized, reported that the doctor gave him a clean bill of health.... Her husband suggested they spend the weekend in the mountains.

"Would you say Ellen had a good or a bad day? According to Ellen, she had a perfectly rotten day, which is how most of her days are. She was convinced her supervisor said yes only because he planned to back out of a promise to hire more clerical help. Her daughter's high grade infuriated her: it confirmed her feeling that the lazy teacher wouldn't give the child an appropriate challenge. Her first reaction to her father's good news was that he was lying, but she had to accept it when she called the doctor to check.... Why bother going away for the weekend? He'd only go off fishing and leave her stuck with the kids."[106]

The events of your day aren't nearly as important as your attitude toward them.

Don't aim for success if you want it; just do what you love and believe in, and it will come naturally.

■■■

*Take delight in the Lord, and he will give you the desires of your heart.*
Psalm 37:4 NRSV

Og Mandino has written: "Every living soul has different talents, different desires, different faculties. Be yourself. Try to be anything else but your genuine self, even if you deceive the entire world, and you will be ten thousand times worse than nothing....

"Consider the plants and the animals of the field, how they live. Does a cotton plant bear even one apple? Does a pomegranate tree ever produce an orange? Does a lion attempt to fly?

"Only man, of all living things, foolishly strives to be other than what he was intended to be....

"You cannot choose your calling. Your calling chooses you. You have been blessed with special skills that are yours alone. Use them, whatever they may be, and forget about wearing another's hat. A talented chariot driver can win gold and renown with his skills. Let him pick figs and he would starve.

"No one can take your place. Realize this and be yourself. You have no obligation to succeed. You have only the obligation to be true to yourself.

"Do the very best that you can, in the things you do best, and you will know, in thy soul, that you are the greatest success in the world."[107]

# Happiness, wealth, and success are by-products...they should not be the goal.

■■■

*Seek first His kingdom*
*and His righteousness; and all these*
*things shall be added to you.*

Matthew 6:33 NASB

The pastor of a church once asked a young boy what he wanted to be when he grew up. The nine-year-old answered, "A returned missionary."

The boy had recently participated in a week-long missionary conference at his church, during which a number of missionaries had spoken. He had viewed their slides, heard their sermons, and taken a close look at their tables filled the artifacts related to their adventures on the mission field.

The boy didn't see the years of study necessary to prepare for the mission field. He didn't know about the years of separation from home, loved ones, and one's own culture. He didn't know what it meant to live mostly routine days in steaming jungles or parched deserts. All he knew was what it meant to return as a missionary and enjoy recognition and acclaim.[108]

Very few people ever reach a goal that brings them happiness, wealth, and a good reputation without first completing a tough set of "preliminary rounds." A musician must practice, an athlete must run, a scientist must experiment, a writer must write, an artist must paint, a farmer must plant.

Choose what you want to be and do *today*. That is what will define your tomorrow.

# Determine that the thing can and shall be done, and then we shall find the way.

■■■

*Is anything too difficult for the Lord?*

Genesis 18:14 NASB

Somebody said that it couldn't be done,
But he with a chuckle replied
That "maybe it couldn't," but he would be one
Who wouldn't say so till he'd tried.
So he buckled right in with the trace of a grin
On his face. If he worried he hid it.
He started to sing as he tackled the thing
That couldn't be done, and he did it.

Somebody scoffed: "Oh, you'll never do that;
At least no one ever has done it";
But he took off his coat and he took off his hat,
And the first thing we knew he'd begun it.
With a lift of his chin and a bit of a grin,
Without any doubting or quiddit,
He started to sing as he tackled the thing
That couldn't be done, and he did it.

There are thousands to tell you it cannot be done,
There are thousands to prophesy failure;
There are thousands to point out to you, one by one,
The dangers that wait to assail you.
But just buckle in with a bit of a grin,
Just take off your coat and go to it;
Just start to sing as you tackle the thing
That "cannot be done," and you'll do it.[109]

—Edgar A. Guest

# Confidence of success often induces real success.

■■■

*Being confident of this very thing, that he which hath begun a good work in you will perform it until the day of Jesus Christ.*

Philippians 1:6 KJV

On the twentieth anniversary of their college graduation, a group of alumni gathered for a reunion. As they reminisced about their college days, they recalled a fellow classmate named Harvey. The thing they remembered most about Harvey was that whenever he was asked what he was going to do after graduation, he said, "I'm going to be a millionaire." His classmates had serious doubts that he would. They remembered him as one of the slowest students in their class. And he was especially poor in mathematics. How could a man expect to make millions if he could hardly add up a column of figures?

As the group was talking about Harvey, guess who pulled up in a brand new, chauffeur-driven Rolls Royce? Harvey stepped out wearing an expensive, tailor-made three-piece suit. His classmates quickly gathered around him and began to ask, "Hey, Harvey, where did you get that car? What happened? How did you do it?"

Harvey said, "Well, I came upon an invention that costs me only five dollars to manufacture and I sell it for one hundred dollars. And you'd be surprised how fast that 10 percent profit adds up!"[110]

An irrepressible self-confidence can be contagious. Don't give up on yourself!

# Falling in love with one's job is the secret of success.

■ ■ ■

*He who finds his life will lose it, and he who loses his life for My sake will find it.*

Matthew 10:39 NKJV

One day, a young minister called upon one of his parishioners — a humble shoemaker who was a devout Christian. He enjoyed talking with the man as he worked and tried to bring the conversation around to the things of God. He said rather ineptly, "How good it is to meet a Christ-like person in such a lowly occupation."

The shoemaker answered, "Brother, I don't consider my occupation to be lowly." The minister, suddenly aware of what he had said and how he had offended the man, said, "Excuse me, my brother, I didn't mean to reflect on what you do to earn a living."

The shoemaker replied, "You didn't hurt me. I believe that my making a pair of shoes is just as great and holy a task as your preaching a sermon. I believe that when I stand before the Lord one day, He will ask me, "What kind of shoes did you make?' and I will be able to tell Him that I made the best shoes I knew to make — ones that I prayed over and made for His glory. I'll tell Him that I prayed, too, for those who would wear my shoes. And He will ask you, 'What kind of messages did you deliver?'"[111]

*How* and *why* we do what we do, matters far more than what we actually do.

# Success lies in this: Do your best. Then expect God's best.

■■■

*All these blessings shall come upon you and overtake you, because you obey the voice of the Lord your God.*

Deuteronomy 28:2 NKJV

While watching the late news one Christmas eve, a minister saw a report on Mother Teresa. She was hugging two AIDS-stricken men who had just been released from prison. The reporter interviewing her asked her why she cared about criminals who had this deadly disease. "They were made in God's image," she said. "They deserve to know that He loves them." The minister admired Mother Teresa's willingness to give of herself to these dying men, but he was also relieved not to be in her shoes. At the time he saw the report little was known about how AIDS was spread and he felt she was putting her life in grave danger.

The next day, the minister was scheduled to preach a Christmas sermon at a nearby women's prison. After he preached, much to his surprise, he was asked to pay a personal call on a prisoner in an isolation cell — she had AIDS. Putting aside his reluctance, he accompanied the prison chaplain to her cell. He found her reading the Bible. After some initial small talk, he asked her, "Do you know Jesus?" She replied that she didn't, but would like to. The minister prayed with her and she accepted Christ as her Savior. Two days later she was released from prison. Three weeks later, she died.[112]

We are each challenged to do what we know is right and then to trust God with the consequences.

The only people who achieve much are those who want knowledge so badly that they seek it while the conditions are still unfavorable.

■ ■ ■

*As the deer pants for the water brooks, so pants my soul for You, O God.*

Psalm 42:1 NKJV

On a hot summer day in 1984, the people in a small New Mexico town watched as a strong young runner passed the Olympic torch to the next runner of the course — nine-year-old Amy. Severely crippled and bent over, Amy had long dreamed of carrying the torch on a leg of its journey from Athens to Los Angeles. When she took the heavy torch, she had to hold it with both hands. She had neither the strength nor agility of the preceding runner. The crowd called out words of encouragement, but few expected her to complete the kilometer.

They didn't know that Amy had a deep desire to complete this challenge. She wanted it more than anything in the world. She and her mother had raised the $3,000 entrance fee by holding bake sales and garage sales in their front yard. Amy had trained for a year with a ten-pound hammer, but never once during that year had she been able to complete the distance. Still, she never gave up trying.

As the crowd cheered, Amy settled into a steady rhythm — slow, but steady nonetheless. To everyone's delight, this time she *did* complete the kilometer. She had literally willed her crippled body to do what seemed impossible for it to do.[113]

How badly do you want to reach *your* goal today?

# You have to want it [success] bad. You can find geniuses on any skid row and average intellects as presidents of banks. It's what pushes you from inside.

■■■

*Do you not know that in a race*
*all the runners run,*
*but only one gets the prize?*
*Run in such a way*
*as to get the prize.*

1 Corinthians 9:24

The tree that never had to fight
For sun and sky and air and light,
That stood out in the open plain
And always got its share of rain,
Never became a forest king,
But lived and died a common thing.
The man who never had to toil,
Who never had to win his share
Of sun and sky and light and air,
Never became a manly man,
But lived and died as he began.

Good timber does not grow on ease
The stronger wind, the tougher trees,
The farther sky, the greater length,
By sun and cold, by rain and snows,
In tree or man good timber grows.
Where thickest stands the forest growth,
We find the patriarchs of both,
And they hold converse with the stars
Whose broken branches show the scars
Of many winds and much of strife,
This is the common law of life.[114]

—Douglas Malloch

Let me tell you
the secret that has
led me to my goal.
My strength lies
solely in my tenacity.

■■■

*When Gideon came to the Jordan,*
*he and the three hundred men*
*who were with him crossed over,*
*exhausted but still in pursuit.*
Judges 8:4 NKJV

Jake Hammack, a teenage swimmer, is deaf. He hears voices as whispers only with the help of hearing aids, which he must take out before he gets into the pool.

In recent months he has found that, "if I keep training hard, I break my times." Hammack now swims "Q" times — the highest standard in Southern California Swimming — in five events. His coach has said, "He's one of the faster swimmers and that's all a matter of hard work. In some ways his handicap may help him. He just charges ahead. He has no distractions."

Hammack loses a little time to opponents at the start of races. "It only bothers me if I don't beat my own times," he says. His times are presently good enough to meet the qualifying standards in seven events for the World Deaf Games, next scheduled for Copenhagen. The idea of such competition is not at all daunting to Hammack. "The guy likes to race," his coach says.

A motivational speaker once brought his pet dog to a seminar. He gave the dog one end of a large steak bone and then grabbed the other end of the bone and tried to pull the bone from the dog's mouth. The dog refused to release his prize. "So, too," the speaker said, "with success. When you want your goal as much as my dog wants this bone, you'll reach it."[115]

# On the clarity of your ideas depends the scope of your success in any endeavor.

■■■

*So I turned my mind to understand, to investigate and to search out wisdom and the scheme of things and to understand the stupidity of wickedness and the madness of folly.*

Ecclesiastes 7:25

Major James Nesmeth, an average weekend golfer shooting in the mid- to low-nineties, dreamed of improving his golf game. But then, for seven years, he never touched a club nor set foot on a fairway. During those years, however, he developed an amazingly effective technique for improving his game. The first time he returned to a course, he shot an astonishing 74! He had cut 20 strokes off his average.

What was his secret? Visualization. For those seven years, Major Nesmeth was a prisoner of war in North Vietnam. He was imprisoned in a cage four-and-a-half feet high and five feet long. Most of those years, he saw no one, talked to no one, and had no physical activity. He knew he had to find some way to occupy his mind or he would lose his sanity, so he began to visualize playing golf. Each day, he played a full 18 holes at the imaginary country club of his dreams. He imagined every detail, every shot. And not once did he miss a shot or putt. Seven days a week, four hours a day, he played eighteen holes in his mind.[116]

Your dreams will be much more likely to come true if you visualize your goals and imagine reaching them. You will be training your mind to produce successful thoughts and ideas.

# The road to success is dotted with many tempting parking places.

■■■

*We want each of you to show this same diligence to the very end, in order to make your hope sure.*

Hebrews 6:11

When Captain Cook and his party set out in search of the North Pole, one of those who was part of the team was Dr. Solander, a Swede who served in the capacity of naturalist. The trip was made in the depth of winter, and a cold south wind accompanied by driving snow caught the party of explorers by surprise while they were some distance from their encampment. Dr. Solander called the men around him and gravely said, "I have had some experience of this in my own country, but you have none. Now, attend to my advice, for upon it depends your lives. We must resolutely set our faces to get back to the encampment, and with never a stop, for the danger lies in falling asleep."

The party leader asked, "I suppose we shall get horribly tired?" Solander replied, "Of course...but it will be a chance to see what we are made of. I warn you...the men, as their blood grows cold, will ask to be allowed to rest. Do not permit it for a moment — urge them — urge them with blows, with the bayonet, if necessary. Remember, the wish to stop is the first symptom of the blood refusing to circulate. To yield to it is death."[117]

The party moved on, and kept moving until all arrived safely at the camp. No one expressed the wish to stop. All had heard, and heeded, Dr. Solander's warning.

# Success results as much from what we don't choose to do as it does from what we choose to do.

■ ■ ■

*I have set before you life or death, blessing or curse. Oh, that you would choose life.*

Deuteronomy 30:19 TLB

In *Taking Chances,* Robert T. Lewis tells the story of Richard Carlyle, a bright, young, aggressive salesman who skyrocketed to the position of national sales manager by the time he was thirty. Soon after, a bad turn in the market caused his company some sudden reverses. Pressure to produce mounted, and Carlyle found that his inexperience prevented him from doing the job required of him. He went to upper management, admitted that he was in over his head, and suggested that he be permitted to find someone to come into the company over him. He offered either to work with the person or resign.

Appreciating his candor and recognizing his potential, they went along with his suggestion. They hired an experienced sales manager who had taken early retirement from another company, and gave him a two-year contract. With coaching from this older, more experienced man, Carlyle acquired the necessary know-how to once again move to the top spot and successfully run the department even before the two years were up.[118]

Carlyle neither denied his failure, nor did he let it demoralize him. He viewed his failure as a sign of inexperience and he addressed the issue constructively.

Failure often sends us a message about what we may need to do or not do. We are wise to listen and learn when necessary.

# Success consists of getting up more times than you fall.

*Though a righteous man falls seven times, he rises again.*

Proverbs 24:16

Ray Charles has been able to do what few musicians can — create music that appeals to young and old, black and white, rich and poor. He successfully crosses major boundaries.

Charles lost both parents and a brother before he was grown. He grew up in a school for the blind, where he learned to play piano and sing. By his late teens, he was a hit in central and north Florida. His friends believed in his talent, and Charles believed in them. In 1946, when Lucky Millinder's band arrived in Orlando, Charles managed to get an audition. It was his first chance at the big time.

Charles sang and played with all his might. Millinder listened quietly. At the end of the audition, as Charles expected to hear praise, all he heard was silence and then finally these devastating words, "Ain't good enough, kid." Charles thought he had heard incorrectly and asked Millinder to repeat what he had said. "You heard me. You don't got what it takes." Charles later said of the incident, "I went back to my room and cried for days."

In retrospect, Charles considers that blow to be the "best thing that ever happened to me. After I got over feeling sorry for myself, I went back and started practicing, so nobody would ever say that about me again."[119]

Everybody takes a hit sometime. The successful bounce back.

# One of the most important lessons of life is that success must continually be won and is never finally achieved.

■■■

*For everyone who keeps on asking receives; and he who keeps on seeking finds; and to him who keeps on knocking, [the door] will be opened.*

Matthew 7:8 AMP

When Apple Computer began to experience financial difficulty, Steven Jobs, Apple's young chairman, traveled to New York City from the company's home base in Silicon Valley. His mission was to convince Pepsico's John Sculley to run the struggling company. As the two men overlooked the Manhattan skyline from Sculley's penthouse office, Jobs made his offer. Sculley responded, "You'd have to give me a million-dollar salary, a million-dollar bonus, and a million-dollar severance." Jobs was stunned, but he agreed — if Sculley would move to California. Sculley would only commit, however, to being a consultant based in New York. At that, Jobs challenged Sculley with a question, "Do you want to spend the rest of your life selling sugared water, or do you want to change the world?"

In his autobiography, *Odyssey,* Sculley writes that Jobs' challenge "knocked the wind out of me." He had become so caught up with his future at Pepsi, his pension, and concerns about how his family might adapt to California, that he had lost sight of a new opportunity, a challenge that he slowly realized was much bigger and more important than his present job.[120]

Success is not found in "arriving," but in constantly pursuing new goals and facing new challenges with all your heart, mind, and soul.

# You may have to fight a battle more than once to win it.

■■■

*Hold on to what you have,*
*so that no one will take your crown.*

Revelation 3:11

When David Yudovin entered the 64° water before dawn, he was trying to complete a journey he had begun nearly twenty years before. In 1978, only 250 yards from the end of a marathon swim near Ventura, California, Yudovin had a near-fatal heart attack. He fought his way back to health and later completed several landmark swims. Now, at age forty-five, he felt ready to take on his supreme challenge, swimming the English Channel.

The odds against a successful channel swim are great. Yudovin had tried three other times and failed. The lure of that twenty-one-plus mile stretch of icy water never left him, though. The swim is dangerous, not only because of the cold water, but because the channel is often laced with sewage, oil slicks, seaweed, jellyfish, and up to four hundred ships a day. On August 20, 1996, the weather reports indicated it was now or never. So he swam. Eight hours into the swim, a storm cell arrived, producing hard rain, strong tidal flow, and extremely choppy water. But Yudovin continued on and when he climbed out of the water near Calais, France, he was elated. "It's so rewarding and so fulfilling it almost tickles inside," he said. His fourth attempt was a victory![121]

Is it time to try again?

# Diligence is the mother of good fortune.

■■■

*The plans of the diligent lead surely to advantage, but everyone who is hasty comes surely to poverty.*

Proverbs 21:5 NASB

The art world is highly competitive and many aspiring artists never succeed in getting their work shown. Kathy Wood, an enamelist, tells how she and her colleagues succeeded: "In 1985 we presented the woman who was in charge of the [Bristol-Myers Squibb] gallery with a portfolio of our work and she turned us down....

"Two years later, hearing that she had left, I proposed the show again, making no reference to our earlier rejection. I was told that the new person would not be starting the job for another six months, and that I should call her in the spring. Then the company underwent a big merger, and I was told I should call again in another few months.... After a few appointments and cancellations we finally got to show the new director of the gallery and her assistant what we had, and they liked it very much but would not commit to a show. Over the next few months...I wrote the director several letters saying how much we'd love to discuss dates for the show, never once mentioning that there had not yet been a firm commitment. Finally, just as we were about to give up, we got a call saying yes, the gallery had decided to give us a show...more than six years after first approaching the gallery. We got a rave review in *The New York Times*."[122]

You haven't failed until you quit knocking at the door!

# Success in life depends upon the three I's: integrity, intelligence, and industry.

■■■

*Keep a clear conscience so that those who speak evil of your good life in Christ will be made ashamed.*

1 Peter 3:16 NCV

Industry, the diligent work that is so frequently linked to success, is very often a daily struggle — a battle against indecision, procrastination, and laziness. The following poem offers an antidote:

We are often greatly bothered
By two fussy little men,
Who sometimes block our pathway —
Their names are How and When.

If we have a task or duty
Which we can put off a while,
And we do not go and do it —
You should see those two rogues smile!

But there is a way to beat them,
And I will tell you how:
If you have a task or duty,
Do it *well*, and do it *now*.

When the submarine *Squalas* and its crew became immobilized on the floor of the Atlantic ocean, a ten-ton diving bell was lowered several times, bringing the thirty-three surviving members of the crew to safety. An observer noted, "Not one of the men said, 'I think I'll wait for another opportunity.'"[123]

Look at every opportunity with a sense of urgency. It may be the missing ingredient that will propel you forward.

# Success is peace of mind, which is a direct result of knowing you did your best to become the best that you are capable of becoming.

■■■

*Do not conform any longer to the pattern of this world, but be transformed by the renewing of your mind. Then you will be able to test and approve what God's will is — his good, pleasing and perfect will.*

Romans 12:2

Stephen Covey, co-author of *First Things First,* once counseled a man whose life he described as, "filled with sloppiness and flakiness." He had a reputation for procrastination and selfishness. He could rarely be counted on to keep his commitments. Covey challenged him to a simple change, "Will you get up in the morning when you say you're planning to get up? Will you just get up in the morning?" The man saw little point in what Covey was challenging him to do. When Covey asked him to commit to getting up at a certain time for a month, the man said, "I really don't know if I can." Covey then asked, "Do you think you could do it for a week?" The man said he thought he could, committed to do so.

Covey saw the man a week later. "Did you do it?" He said, "I did!" Covey then asked, "Now, what's the next thing you're going to commit to do?" Little by little, the man began to make and keep commitments. No one else knew of the plan but Covey and one friend who encouraged him. Over time, the man made remarkable changes. His emotions became stable, his promises were kept, his integrity was regained, and his relationships improved.[124]

Integrity begins with being true to yourself. When you keep your word to you, it becomes easier to keep your word to others, which produces tremendous peace of mind.

# The secret of success is to be like a duck — smooth and unruffled on the top, but paddling furiously underneath.

■■■

*Better a patient man than a warrior,*
*a man who controls his temper*
*than one who takes a city.*

Proverbs 16:32

Ellen Burstyn, a Tony Award-winning actress, once had a memorable acting lesson that she enjoys relating to those who question her about stage fright:

"One day on Broadway, I became aware of a stir in the audience. Suddenly, I saw it! A stray cat was nonchalantly crossing the stage.

"The cat stopped and turned toward the darkness of the audience and seemed startled to discover that the darkness was alive. She had presence, as though there were a thousand pairs of eyes out there, which, of course, there were. That realization stopped the cat dead in her tracks. Then she fled into the wings. I remember thinking, *I know just how she feels.*

"I've often told the story to young actors because I think it shows that the job of the actor is: to make contact with the kitty inside each of us that wants to turn and run when we feel those thousand pairs of eyes on us. And to find the way to quiet the kitty and just go on doing what we have to do."[125]

Feeling frightened or nervous is not a sign of impending failure. It is a sign that you consider the performance ahead to be worth doing and doing well! Keep your eyes on your goal and remember those who will benefit from your work. This focus will calm your fears and fill you with purpose.

If A is success in life, then A equals x plus y plus z. Work is x, y is play, and z is keeping your mouth shut.

■■■

*Those who are careful about what they say keep themselves out of trouble.*

Proverbs 21:23 NCV

Although their religious heritage is one marked by emotional response and physical manifestations of God's power, the Quakers are generally regarded as being very reserved in their everyday dealings with other people. One of the most famous Quakers, William Penn, was a strong advocate for speaking only when one had something important to say. He once gave this advice:

"Avoid company where it is not profitable or necessary, and in those occasions, speak little, and last. Silence is wisdom where speaking is folly, and always safe. Some are so foolish as to interrupt and anticipate those who speak instead of hearing and thinking before they answer, which is uncivil, as well as silly. If thou thinkest twice before thou speakest once, thou wilt speak twice the better for it. Better to say nothing than not to the purpose. And to speak pertinently, consider both what is fit, and when it is fit, to speak. In all debates, let truth be thy aim, not victory or an unjust interest; and endeavor to gain, rather than to expose, thy antagonist."[126]

Sam Rayburn had this abbreviated version of the same advice: "The unspoken word never defeats one. What one does not say does not have to be explained."

Guard your words closely, both at work and at play.

# A great secret of success is to go through life as a man who never gets used up.

■■■

*But they that wait upon the Lord shall renew their strength; they shall mount up with wings as eagles; they shall run, and not be weary; and they shall walk, and not faint.*

Isaiah 40:31 KJV

As a consequence of being nominated to serve on the National Council on Disability, Joni Eareckson Tada was required to be fingerprinted by the FBI. She writes in *Glorious Intruder*: "The polite G-man had problems with me. Yes, I cooperated to the best of my ability, but have you ever tried fingerprinting a lady who hasn't used her fingers in twenty years?...The poor agent had one big headache trying to get prints off the pads of my fingers. Finally, after four or five tries, he looked at me, shook his head and said, 'Lady, I'm sorry, but you just don't have any tread on these fingers of yours.'"

The agent then turned her hand over so she could get a close look at her own fingers. She discovered that the pads of her fingers were smooth. Joni asked the agent if he had run into this before. He said, "No," and explained that the only folks without prints are those who never use their hands. The ridges on fingers deepen with use. The hands of bricklayers, carpenters, typists, and homemakers who do a lot of dishes always have good prints.

Tada notes, "I would have thought just the opposite. It seemed to me that hard work would wear off good fingerprints. But not so. Hard work enhances them."[127]

Success is not
the result of
spontaneous
combustion.
You must
set yourself
on fire.

■■■

*For this reason I remind you*
*to fan into flame the gift of God.*

2 Timothy 1:6

John Wesley, the founder of Methodism, had a contagious enthusiasm for his work. With a singleness of purpose, he had an inner burning desire to be the best possible instrument he could be for the Lord's work.

A small man, weighing only about 127 pounds, he rose each morning at 5 a.m., and every day rode by horseback through the English countryside, seeking out people to hear his message. Some days he rode up to sixty miles in a day, quite an accomplishment at that time. Many nights, he could still be found preaching at midnight — energetic, enthusiastic, unexhausted.

Twelve thousand people once heard John Wesley preach all day. They came by foot, oxcart, horseback, and carriage to the open air meeting.

Once, a man was so touched by Wesley's message that he rushed through the crowd, grabbed Wesley, and said, "Dr. Wesley, you're a phenomenal speaker. Thousands came here today to hear you speak. What's your secret?"

Wesley replied, "I don't know, son. I just set John Wesley on fire, and people come to see him burn!"[128]

Stir up the gift that is within you. Fan the coals to flame! Then go spread your fire to those who need it.

# The difference between failure and success is doing a thing nearly right and doing it exactly right.

■■■

*The wicked man does deceptive work,*
*but he who sows righteousness*
*will have a sure reward.*

Proverbs 11:18 NKJV

While Mike Kollin was a linebacker for the Miami Dolphins, his former college coach — Shug Jordan of Auburn University — asked him to do some recruiting for him. Mike said, "Sure, coach. What kind of player are you looking for?"

Jordan replied, "Well, Mike, you know there's that fellow, you knock him down, he just stays down?" Mike said, "We don't want him, do we, coach?"

"No, that's right," the coach said. "Then there's that fellow, you knock him down and he gets up, but you knock him down again and he stays down." Mike responded, "We don't want him either, do we, coach?"

Jordan said, "No, but Mike, there's a fellow, you knock him down, he gets up. Knock him down, he gets up. Knock him down, he gets up. Knock him down, he gets up." Mike responded enthusiastically, "That's the guy we want, isn't it, coach?"

The coach answered, "No, we don't want him either. I want you to find that guy who's knocking everybody down. That's the guy we want!"[129]

The key to success lies not only in doing good work, but in getting the job done.

# Make yourself indispensable and you'll be moved up. Act as if you're indispensable and you'll be moved out.

■■■

*Solomon, seeing that the young man was industrious, made him the officer over all the labor force of the house of Joseph.*

1 Kings 11:28 NKJV

John made average grades in his college business courses but after graduation, he managed to land a good job with a major company. A handsome young man, well-dressed, well-mannered, and driving a stylish car, he made an excellent impression when he called on clients. What John did not realize was that his supervisor had hired him for just that purpose — he labeled John's job a "face job" — one aimed at maintaining corporate contact and sending the message, "We care and we're here" — but he expected very little from John in the way of production.

John's goal, however, was to move up, not simply remain "out front." When he called on clients, he not only got to know them socially and professionally, but he asked the right questions: *What needs do you have?* and *How might our company help you further?* His clients not only appreciated his concern, but responded positively to his proposals and quotes for new business. Within a year, John was the top producer in his department. His supervisor was stunned — he had hired John only to maintain the status quo, something he himself had become quite adept at doing. He was even more stunned when six months later, John was given his job.

A job is what you are given. A career is what you make of your job.

# I have never believed that any success outside the home can compensate for failure within it.

■■■

*Blessed is the man who fears the Lord, who finds great delight in his commands. His children will be mighty in the land.*

Psalm 112:1,2

In *From Bad Beginnings to Happy Endings*, Ed Young writes: "I know a family that has six boys, all fine young men now and away from the nest. People used to tell this father, 'Boy, I'd give any amount of money if I could have raised six young men as fine as yours.' Wesley Neely had his own thriving lumber business, and it supported the family comfortably. I believe that with his skill and drive he could have been a millionaire, but his business never really skyrocketed like everyone thought it could. The reason? Rather than devote endless time and energy to work, he chose to spend more hours with his sons, especially when they were young.

"His choices cost him money, but oh, what he gained! The money Wesley did make wasn't spent on personal hobbies and pleasures. He was much more interested in cultivating his children than accruing capital. True fatherhood is costly — and the currency of parenting is called time."

In an unfinished letter found after his death, Michael Landon stated, "A man's family is everything." Too often, people intent upon personal success fail to understand that. It means nothing if you lose your family in the process.[130]

# If you want to learn about success, listen to someone who has succeeded.

■■■

*Hear, O sons, the instruction of a father, and give attention that you may gain understanding, for I give you sound teaching.*

Proverbs 4:1,2 NASB

When Sam Findley decided it was time to retire from the garment business, he called his son Mervyn into his office to give him the news. He gave his son this bit of advice: "Son, it's all yours. I've made a success of this business because of two principles: reliability and wisdom. First, take reliability. If you promise goods by the tenth of the month, no matter what happens, you must deliver by the tenth. Even if it costs you overtime, double time, golden time. You deliver what you promise."

Mervyn pondered his father's advice for a few moments and then asked, "What about wisdom?" His father shot back: "Wisdom is never making such a stupid promise."[131]

Very often we learn from others what *to* do. At times, we learn what *not* to do. Both are valuable lessons.

The most important lessons, however, are not likely to be the ones we hear from others, or even the ones we gain by observing their lives. Rather, they are the lessons we learn for ourselves, as the result of our own accomplishments and failures. Never count a setback as a loss, *unless* you fail to learn from it. Listen, too, to the message of your own successes. You are likely to hear the drumbeat of work, values, quality, and persistence.

# Before everything else, getting ready is the secret of success.

■■■

*Suppose one of you wants to build a tower. Will he not first sit down and estimate the cost to see if he has enough money to complete it?*

Luke 14:28

British explorer David Livingstone once wrote the following about his preparations for an African expedition: "The only important thing to be done at Zanzibar was to buy certain provisions — such as flour, rice, and tinned meat — and to decide what to take in the way of beads, cloth, and brass wire, which were used as currency with the natives in the interior. The choice was difficult, since one tribe valued one kind of bead or cloth, while its neighbour would only accept something quite different. If the traveller were without the right sort of commodity he could buy nothing, and there were many things, such as milk, vegetables, and eggs, which were essential; also he could go no farther, since each tribe levied a tribute and, without the right quantity of the right goods, paid in full, he was refused permission to cross their territory. For a journey of any length this necessitated an enormous quantity of goods, which had to be carried by native porters recruited on the coast. But an expedition also had to have a guard, made up of natives of a higher quality than the porters, and these were enlisted in Zanzibar."[132]

The process of getting ready for an important project or performance can often require the majority of effort and investment. Preparation, however, dictates performance.

# Success is achieving the goals you have set for yourself.

■■■

*But the noble man devises noble plans;*
*and by noble plans he stands.*

Isaiah 32:8 NASB

A woman named Sue had fairly serious health problems. An invalid since childhood, she had a birth defect that left a hole in one of the chambers of her heart. The births of five children, a number of surgeries, and a weight gain all took their toll. She lived in almost constant pain. Then she decided that one of the things she wanted to do most in life was to run a marathon, a feat her friends and husband thought was totally unrealistic. She became committed to her goal, however, and began running, very slowly, in the subdivision where they lived. Each day she ran just a little further. Soon she was running one mile, then three, then five. Finally, Sue registered to run in a marathon.

Sue ran a smart race — stopping regularly to stretch, drinking plenty of water, and pacing herself. The race was run mostly in the rain, however, and when no more runners were seen crossing the finish line, Sue's family became concerned. Her husband went in search of her. He found her a couple of miles from the finish, encouraging a group of friends with whom she was running. She crossed the finish line five-and-a-half hours after starting the race, but she finished! Her goal had been reached![133]

Our goals change us. Reaching them establishes us.

# I cannot give you the formula for success but I can give you the formula for failure — which is: Try to please everyone.

■■■

*Am I now trying to win the approval of men, or of God? Or am I trying to please men? If I were still trying to please men, I would not be a servant of Christ.*

Galatians 1:10

George Jones began his career as a clerk in a crockery store. He gained a reputation as a bright, energetic, and honest young man. Because of his good habits, correct deportment, and affable manners, the great journalist Henry J. Raymond became interested in having him as a partner. Together, Jones and Raymond started *The New York Times*.

Jones proved himself to be an indefatigable worker. He had an unswerving fidelity to duty and his honesty became conspicuous in the city. *The Times* took on the corruption it found in New York's city politics, and in particular, the corruption in the infamous Tweed dynasty. Report after report brought various aspects of their immoral behavior to light. At one point, Jones was offered $5 million to retire to Europe.

"Yes," said Jones to the offer, and then quickly added the assurance of his adamant refusal, "and know myself for a rascal." He refused to participate, even when the price was more than he ever hoped to earn the rest of his life.[134]

The only One you can ever please fully is the only One who is worth pleasing at all: The Lord God Almighty.

# There are no secrets to success. It is the result of preparation, hard work, learning from failure.

■■■

*Sow for yourselves righteousness,*
*reap the fruit of unfailing love,*
*and break up your unplowed ground;*
*for it is time to seek the Lord.*

Hosea 10:12

Many years ago there was a famous Japanese artist named Hokusai, whose paintings were coveted by royalty. One day, a nobleman commissioned a painting of his prized bird. He left the bird with Hokusai and the artist told him to return in a week.

The nobleman missed his beautiful bird and was anxious to return at the end of the week, not only to pick up his favorite pet, but also his painting. When the nobleman arrived, the artist humbly requested a two-week postponement. The two-week delay stretched into two months, then six. Finally, a year later the nobleman stormed into Hokusai's studio. He refused to wait any longer and demanded both his bird and his painting. Hokusai bowed to the nobleman and turned to his workshop table. He picked up a brush and large sheet of rice paper, and within moments, had effortlessly painted an exact likeness of the lovely bird.

The nobleman was stunned, and then angry. "Why did you keep me waiting for a year if you could have done the painting in such a short time?" he demanded. Hokusai replied, "You don't understand." He then escorted the man into a room where the walls were covered with paintings of the same bird. None of them were as fine as the final rendering. They had all amounted to practice.[135]

Nothing of real value comes easily.

It is always easy to covet another man's success without envying his labors.

■■■

*All hard work brings a profit,*
*but mere talk leads only to poverty.*

Proverbs 14:23

Each night, millions of Americans watch late-night talk shows. The founder of that format is generally regarded to be Steve Allen, whose comedic talk show was created in 1953, and first went on the air in 1954 as "The Tonight Show."

Allen began his career in radio. He was the author of two poetry anthologies, two short-story collections, and several novels. He was an accomplished pianist and lyricist who wrote more than 4,000 songs, including scores for Broadway plays. In addition, he was a popular lecturer, and wrote the "Meeting of the Minds" series for PBS television.

Many people would like to trade lives with someone of Allen's creativity and success. What many of Allen's admirers don't know, however, is that he had an abusive mother who often vented her vicious temper on him. Throughout his childhood he stayed with dozens of alcoholic aunts and uncles, and attended 18 schools before graduating from high school. At age 13, he ran away from home to seek an aunt in California, riding his bicycle most of the way until it finally broke down. He continued his journey on freight trains, eating ant-covered leftovers that wandering hoboes left behind.[136]

It's easy to reach for success, but it can be difficult to embrace the failures and problems that can push us toward our goals.

# Try not to become a man of success but rather try to become a man of value.

■■■

*Turn my heart to your decrees, and not to selfish gain.*

Psalm 119:36 NRSV

When Jewish psychiatrist Victor Frankl, author of the classic best-seller *Man's Search for Meaning*, was arrested by the Nazis in World War II, he was stripped of everything: family, possessions, property. Even a manuscript on which he had worked for years, was ripped from the lining of his coat and discarded. He later said, "It seemed as if nothing and no one would survive me; neither a physical nor a spiritual child of my own! I found myself confronted with the question of whether under such circumstances my life was ultimately void of any meaning."

A few days later, Nazis forced the prisoners to give up their clothes. In return, Frankl was given the rags of an inmate who had been sent to the gas chamber. In the pocket of his "new" coat, he found a single page torn out of a Hebrew prayer book. It contained the main Jewish prayer, *Shema Yisrael* ("Hear, O Israel! The Lord our God is one God. And you shall love the Lord your God with all your heart and with all your soul and with all your might.") Frankl found a *why* for living, and in the process, discovered that "he who has a why to live for can bear almost any how." That premise gave him the courage, inspiration, and reason to survive.[137]

Take a look at *why* you live today. It determines greatly *what* you choose to do and *how* you choose to live.

# Small numbers make no difference to God. There is nothing small if God is in it.

■■■

*If you have faith as a mustard seed, you shall say to this mountain, "Move from here to there," and it shall move; and nothing shall be impossible to you.*

Matthew 17:20 NASB

A well-known minister was invited to be the guest speaker at a church in another state. He was met at the airport by the young pastor of the church. As they drove along, the well-known minister asked the young pastor, "How are things going in your church?"

The pastor replied, "We've been through it lately." After a brief pause, he added, "In fact, we've cut our membership a bit...to be precise, we've cut our congregation in half."

"What happened?" the visitor asked. The pastor responded, "We had more than 200 members, but nothing was happening. The place was dead. No matter what I preached, nothing changed. So one day the deacons and I prayed, 'Lord, bring only Your people here. We want those who are ready to give themselves wholly to You.' We stood at the door of the church and prayed this silently as people filed in. And an amazing thing happened. People began dropping out, one by one. We went down to about 100. Then the place began to change. We almost went broke, but people got serious with God and started getting involved. Membership is creeping back up. I believe we're on the brink of revival!"[138]

It's not the starting point that counts but rather, the *eternal* result.

# It is not enough to begin; continuance is necessary. Success depends upon staying power.

■■■

*Be steadfast, immovable, always abounding in the work of the Lord, knowing that your labor is not in vain in the Lord.*

1 Corinthians 15:58 NKJV

estaments we read today were only made by the faithful work of manuscript copyists the centuries. While we do not have the original manuscripts, we do have over 99.9 percent of the original text.

Copying was a long and arduous process before the invention of the printing press. It was not customary for copyists to sit at a table or desk. Scribes usually stood while making notes, or sat on a stool or bench (even the ground), holding their scroll on their knees. Something of the hard work involved has been gleaned from the notes scribes have placed at the close of their scrolls:

"He who does not know how to write supposes it to be no labor; but though only three fingers write, the whole body labors."

"Writing bows one's back, thrusts the ribs into one's stomach, and fosters a general debility of the body."

One Armenian manuscript of the Gospels indicates that it was copied during a raging snowstorm — the scribe's ink froze, his hand became numb, and the pen fell from his fingers.

This good news has also been noted, however: "There is no scribe who will not pass away, but what his hands have written will remain forever."[139]

It is a deep-seated belief on the part of almost all Americans that their success will be better assured as they help to build the success of others.

*Each of you should look not only to your own interests, but also to the interests of others.*

Philippians 2:4

The complex shapes and infinite uniqueness of snowflakes have confounded scientists for centuries. In the past, scientists believed that the making of a snowflake was a two-step process: the making of a single crystal and then its growth. The process begins as a microscopic speck of dust is trapped in a molecule of water vapor inside the winds of a winter storm. The particle is frosted with droplets of super-cooled water, becomes heavier, and begins to plunge to earth. The icy crystal is sculpted by the varying temperature and humidity it encounters as it falls.

In recent decades, however, a mystery was uncovered. Scientists discovered that very few snowflakes contained a speck of dust or other particle. How were the majority of flakes formed? Dr. John Hallett, a physicist at the University of Nevada, discovered the answer. As snowflakes are formed, extremely dry or cold air causes them to break up into smaller parts. The small fragments then act as seeds for new flakes to develop. Most of snow is made, therefore, by snow![140]

In like manner, successful people generally owe their success to those who have inspired and motivated them. Choose your mentors wisely. Then, choose to mentor others.

# Success is to be measured not by wealth, power, or fame, but by the ratio between what a man is and what he might be.

■■■

*The Lord judges the peoples; judge me, O Lord, according to my righteousness and according to the integrity that is in me.*

Psalm 7:8 NRSV

Johnny Baker grew up in Meridian, Mississippi, and attended Mississippi State on a football scholarship. He went on to play professional ball for the Houston Oilers and the San Diego Chargers.

Following his retirement from professional football, he began to work in investments and real estate. Johnny has been richly blessed with material success, but his greater reputation is as a giver who has been very generous to his church and countless individuals.

The most accurate information about Johnny might come from the shoe shine man at the country club where Johnny plays golf. He knows Johnny as the man who calls him "sir" out of respect for his age. He says that while most folks just toss their shoes at him and expect a job well done, Johnny takes time to talk to him as if he *is* somebody, because to Johnny he is! You might also hear good things about Johnny from the hundred members of the adult Sunday school class he co-teaches, or ask his wife and four children. Johnny Baker has a strong reputation for treating "nobodies" and "somebodies" the same.[141]

Who you are is always reflected in the way you treat others. That is the foundation for integrity, the true measure of character, the true indicator of success.

# The bridge between failure and success is hope.

■■■

*Happy is he...whose hope is in the Lord his God.*

Psalm 146:5 NKJV

In her early days in New York, struggling to launch a theater career, Carol Burnett was called to audition for a revival of Rodgers and Hart's *Babes in Arms*. She felt her dreams were about to come true. She had imagined for years that the legendary Broadway playwright and director George Abbott would be her first director, but she was grateful for any part she might get. Her audition came, and went. In her own words, Burnett "was awful."

Carol returned to her apartment where her sister Chrissy was hoping to hear good news. Carol described what happened and burst into tears. Her sister gave her a hug and cheered her with these words of hope, "One door closes, another one opens." By dinnertime, she had raised Burnett's spirits so that she was laughing when the phone rang. It was a call for another audition — this time for the lead in *Once Upon a Mattress*, directed by George Abbott! Burnett got the lead role she had always dreamed of.[142]

Thornton Wilder once noted, "Hope is a projection of the imagination.... In response to hope the imagination is aroused to picture every possible issue, to try every door, to fit together even the most heterogeneous pieces in the puzzle."[143] Choose to be hopeful today. It is the best self-motivator possible.

# How you *define* success determines to a great extent whether you succeed.

■■■

*Then Job answered the Lord, and said, I know that thou canst do every thing...So the Lord blessed the latter end of Job more than his beginning.*

Job 42:1,2,12 KJV

The story is told of an organization out West that offered a bounty of $5,000 for each wolf captured alive. Sam and Jed decided that this was a great deal. They saw a tremendous opportunity to strike it rich, just as their prospecting ancestors of old had done. They outfitted themselves for the challenge and then hiked into the area. For weeks, they spent day and night scouring the mountains and forests in search of their valuable prey.

Late one night, exhausted, they fell asleep and began to dream of their potential fortune. Sam suddenly awoke with a start, and rubbed his eyes. He wasn't entirely sure if he was awake or dreaming, but then suddenly realized that, indeed, he was awake! At the edges of the firelight cast from their campfire, he saw that he and Jed were surrounded by about fifty wolves — each with flaming eyes and bared teeth.

He nudged his friend to awaken him, crying, "Jed, wake up! We're rich!"[144]

Your definition of success is a prerequisite for setting goals, making plans, and developing methods and timetables for implementing your plans. What you define is likely to be what you achieve. Are you sure you truly want to do that work and become that person?

# To find his place and fill it is success for a man.

■■■

*Desire that ye might be filled*
*with the knowledge of his will in all*
*wisdom and spiritual understanding;*
*that ye might walk worthy*
*of the Lord unto all pleasing,*
*being fruitful in every good work.*

Colossians 1:9,10 KJV

Mike Jordan made a good living from the service station he owned, but he had trouble finding good mechanics to work for him. One day his wife told him to stop complaining about the problem and do something to fix it. With a mechanic's heart for "fixing things," he did just that. He went back to school, earned his teaching credential, and began teaching high school auto shop.

In his first year of teaching, Jordan made less than $10,000. As a gas station owner, he could make that much in a month. "But I wasn't happy owning a station," he has said. "I'm happy doing this." Jordan has found a great deal of personal satisfaction in the success of his students.

Since 1949, California has held a statewide high school auto mechanics contest. In 1996, a two-girl team coached by Jordan won the contest. It was a first in the contest's history. Many of Jordan's former students are working at auto dealerships all across the nation.

Regardless of what you are earning or achieving, if the field in which you are performing is not what you enjoy and doesn't give you a deep sense of meaning and personal satisfaction, you aren't truly succeeding in fulfilling your purpose. Go with what brings satisfaction to your heart. The rewards will be just what you have always desired.

# He has achieved success who has lived well, laughed often, and loved much.

■■■

*I know the best thing we can do is always to enjoy life.*

Ecclesiastes 3:12 CEV

Milton lived a normal, happy childhood and when he was fifteen, he became an apprentice to a candy maker — a job he loved from the very first day. Four years later, he opened his own candy store. The long hours required to make a new business a success took their toll, however, and Milton was forced to close his business because of his failing health. At twenty-six, Milton moved to New York, to work in a candy store again. This time he was a delivery man. When his horse bolted one day and spilled his wagon of candy, Milton was fired. He moved home to Pennsylvania.

Since candy making was the only occupation that interested him, he rented an abandoned factory and started making his own. At first, he made only caramels, then when machinery made it possible to mass produce a single chocolate item, he switched to chocolate. At age forty-six, Milton Hershey broke ground for his first chocolate factory. Within a few years he was a millionaire.

In 1910, Hershey opened a school and offered poor boys a chance to learn a trade. When each boy graduated, Hershey gave him a hundred dollars to begin his career. Tens of thousands of boys got their start in life because a loving, caring man lost himself in generosity.[145]

Hershey loved candy and people. They were his only true interests. What are yours?

And I can live
my life on earth
Contented to the end,
If but a few shall
know my worth
And proudly
call me friend.

■■■

*Bear ye one another's burdens,*
*and so fulfill the law of Christ.*

Galatians 6:2 KJV

Let me live in a house by the side of the road,
Where the race of men go by —
The men who are good and the men who are bad,
As good and as bad as I.
I would not sit in the scorner's seat,
Or hurl the cynic's ban;
Let me live in a house by the side of the road
And be a friend to man.

I see from my house by the side of the road,
By the side of the highway of life,
The men who press with the ardor of hope,
The men who are faint with the strife.
But I turn not away from their smiles nor their tears
— Both parts of an infinite plan;
Let me live in my house by the side of the road
And be a friend to man.

Let me live in a house by the side of the road,
Where the race of men go by —
They are good, they are bad, they are weak,
they are strong. Wise, foolish — so am I.
Then why should I sit in the scorner's seat
Or hurl the cynic's ban? —
Let me live in my house by the side of the road
And be a friend to man.[146]

—Sam Walter Foss

# Success is seeking, knowing, loving and obeying God. If you seek, you will know; if you know, you will love; if you love, you will obey.

■■■

*Grace and peace be multiplied unto you through the knowledge of God, and of Jesus our Lord, according as his divine power hath given unto us all things that pertain unto life and godliness, through the knowledge of him that hath called us to glory and virtue.*

2 Peter 1:2,3 KJV

A young Sunday school teacher shocked her Christian friends one evening when she said, "Four years ago this week, a young girl sat crying on the floor of a New Jersey apartment, devastated by the news of a lab report. Unmarried and alone, she had just learned she was pregnant." She continued, "I had found out about Christ while in the drug scene. After I learned about Him, I knew I wanted to commit myself to Him, but I couldn't give up my old friends or my old habits.... Being pregnant ripped through the hypocrisy of my double life." She then related how she had sought an abortion with the full support of her parents and boyfriend.

She said, "I was looking out my bedroom window one night when...I realized I either believed this Christianity or I didn't believe it. And if I believed in Christ, then I couldn't do this.... That decision was a point of no return." She had her baby, named her Sarah, and allowed a childless Christian couple to adopt her.

She concluded her testimony, "I thought in the depths of my despair that my life was ruined, but I knew I had to at least be obedient...because of that very despair and obedience, I have what I never thought I could — a godly husband and now a baby of our own."[147]

True success is obeying God.

# References

# Acknowledgments

Charles Colson (10), Booker T. Washington (12), Baron Pierre de Coubertin (14), Thomas Jefferson (16), Helen Keller (18), Grantland Rice (22), English Proverb (24), Charles Buxton (26), Logan Pearsall Smith (28), Vince Lombardi (30), Thomas Carlyle (32), Corrie ten Boom (36), H.M. Field (38), Norman Vincent Peale (40), Chapin (44), C.W. Wendte (46), Ron Dentinger (48), Harry J. Kaiser (50), Herschel Walker (52), Loretta Lynn (54), Huey P. Long (56), T.T. Munger (60), George Washington Carver (62), W.E.B. Du Bois (64), Carl Sandburg (68), Ben Azzai (70), An Wang (72), Bear Bryant (74), B.C. Forbes (76), Arthur Ashe (78), William Menninger (80), Henry P. Davison (82), Wofford B. Camp (84), Joseph French Johnson (86), Henry Ford (88,274), John Greenleaf Whittier (90), Homer (92), Charles "Tremendous" Jones (94,168), Dr. Frank Crane (96), Richard Brinsley Sheridan (98), Sammy Kershaw (100), A.T. Mercie (102), Charles Kendall Adams (104), Henry Ward Beecher (106,142,190), Joseph Addison (108), H.W. Arnold (110), Stewart E. White (112), Arthur Helps (114),

Philip Chesterfield (116), Marie Dressler (118), Vesta M. Kelly (120), Bob Brown (122), Charles-Lewis de Secondant, Bardon de Montesquieu (124), William J.H. Boetcker (126), John Stevenson (128), Denis Waitely and Reni Witt (130), O. Byron Cooper (132), Dolly Parton (136), Pendar (140), Ann Landers (144), Thomas Fuller (146), Wilson Mizner (148), George Sand (150), Theodore Roosevelt (152), C. Malesherbez (156), James Gordon Bennett (158), George F. Tilton (160), A.L. Williams (162), Leigh Mitchell Hodges (164), Jonathan Winters (166), Beverly Sills (170), E.H. Harriman (174), John Hayes Hammond (176), Eddie Cantor,(178), William Shakespeare (180), Helen Hayes (182), Anna Pavlova (184), William A. Ward (192), Oswald Spengler (194), Henry Wadsworth Longfellow (198), Larry Bird (200), Joseph Heller (204), Marvin Feldman (206), Donald Riggs (212), Jackie Sherrill (214), Francis Bacon (216), Albert Hubbard (218), David Frost (222), Abraham Lincoln (226), Sigmund Freud (228), Oral Roberts (232), C.S. Lewis (234), Charley Winner (236), Louis Pasteur (238), James Robertson (240), Oliver Goldsmith (246), Charles Evans Hughes (248), Margaret Thatcher (250), Miguel de Cervantes (252), Charles Rupert Stockard (254), John Wooden (256), Albert Einstein (260,284), Albert

# Endnotes

[1]*The Transforming Power of Prayer*, John Houston (Colorado Springs, CO: NavPress, 1996), pp. 111,112.

[2]*Illustrations for Preaching & Teaching*, Craig Brian Larson (Grand Rapids, MI: Baker Books, 1993), p. 63.

[3]*You Can Excel in Times of Change*, Shad Helmstetter (New York: Pocket Books (Simon & Schuster), 1991), p. 167.

[4]*One Door Closes, Another Door Opens*, Arthur Pine (NY: Dell Trade Paperback, 1993), pp. 2,3.

[5]*The Book of Virtues*, William J. Bennett, ed. (New York: Simon & Schuster, 1993), p. 536.

[6]*Taking Chances*, Robert T. Lewis (Boston: Houghton Mifflin Co., 1979), pp. 167,168.

[7]*Reader's Digest*, March 1994, pp. 116,117.

[8]*Illustrations Unlimited*, James Hewett, ed. (Wheaton, IL: Tyndale House, 1988), p. 467.

[9]*The 10 Natural Laws of Successful Time and Life Management*, Hyrum W. Smith (NY: Warner Books, 1994), p. 25.

[10]*Profiles of Genius*, Gene N. Landrum (Buffalo, NY: Prometheus Books, 1993), p. 15.

[11]*Women Who Made a Difference*, Malcolm Forbes (NY: Simon & Schuster, 1990), pp. 166-169.

[12]*Reader's Digest*, September 1996, pp. 126-131.

[13]*Bible Power for Successful Living*, Norman Vincent Peale (Grand Rapids, MI: Fleming H. Revell, 1993), pp. 127,128.

[14]*Dr. Livingstone, I Presume?* Ian Anstruther (NY: E.P. Dutton & Co., 1957), pp. 44-47 and David Livingstone — Explorer and Prophet, Charles J. Finger (NY: Doubleday, Doran & Co. 1927), pp. 254-257.

[15]*One Door Closes, Another Door Opens*, Arthur Pine (New York: Dell Trade Paperback, 1993), pp. 26-29.

[16]*Illustrations for Preaching & Teaching*, Craig Brian Larson (Grand Rapids, MI: Baker Books, 1993), p. 96.

[17]*Design for Living*, Clinton T. Howell (NY: Grosset & Dunlap, 1970), p. 39.

[18]*Reader's Digest*, December 1995, pp. 68-73.

[19]*Straight A's Never Made Anybody Rich*, Wess Roberts (NY: HarperCollins, 1991), pp. 168,169.

[20]*One Door Closes, Another Door Opens*, Arthur Pine (NY: Dell Trade Paperback, 1993), pp. 85-87.

[21]*Illustrations Unlimited*, James Hewett (Wheaton, IL: Tyndale House, 1988), p. 469.

[22]*The Seven Habits of Highly Successful People*, Stephen R. Covey (NY: Simon & Schuster, 1989), p. 214.

[23]*Illustrations Unlimited*, James S. Hewett, ed. (Wheaton, IL: Tyndale, 1988), pp. 59,60.

[24]*Encyclopedia of 7700 Illustrations*, Paul Lee Tan. ed. (Rockville, MD: Assurance Publishers, 1979), pp. 1386 and 1508.

[25]*Design for Living*, Clinton T. Howell (NY: Grosset & Dunlap, 1970), p. 103.

[26]*Illustrations Unlimited*, James S. Hewett, ed. (Wheaton, IL: Tyndale, 1988), p. 57.

[27]*Encyclopedia of 7700 Illustrations*, Paul Lee Tan, ed. (Rockville, MD: Assurance Publishers, 1979), pp. 687,688.

[28]*San Luis Obispo County Telegram-Tribune*, September 6, 1996, p. C2 and September 7, 1996 p. C2.

[29]*Reader's Digest*, June 1987, pp. 110-112.

[30]*Bible Power for Successful Living*, Norman Vincent Peale (Grand Rapids, MI: Fleming H. Revell, 1993), p. 87.

[31]*Sin, Sex and Self-Control*, Norman Vincent Peale (NY: Doubleday & Co., Inc., 1965), p. 25.

[32]*Reader's Digest*, February, 1994, p. 119.

[33]*Encyclopedia of 7700 Illustrations*, Paul Lee Tan, ed. (Rockville, MD: Assurance Publishers, 1979), pp. 474,475.

[34]*Norman Vincent Peale's Treasury of Courage and Confidence*, Norman Vincent Peale, ed. (Garden City, NY: Doubleday & Co., 1970), pp. 190,191.

[35]*Illustrations Unlimited*, James S. Hewett, ed. (Wheaton, IL: Tyndale, 1988), pp. 131,132.

[36]*They Rose Above It*, Bob Consodine (Garden City, NY: Doubleday & Co., 1977), p. 9.

[37]*Reader's Digest*, March 1996, pp. 106,107.

[38]*God's Joyful Runner*, Russell W. Ramsey (South Plainfield, NJ: Bridge Publishing Co., 1987), pp. 3-68.

[39]*Illustrations for Preaching and Teaching*, Craig Brian Larson (Grand Rapids, Baker Books, 1993), p. 34.

[40]*The 10 Natural Laws of Successful Time and Life Management*, Hyrum W. Smith (NY: Warner Books, 1994), pp. 60-70.

[41]*It's Always Too Soon to Quit*, Lewis R. Timberlake (Grand Rapids, MI: Fleming H. Revell, 1988), pp. 100,101.

[42]*Encyclopedia of 7700 Illustrations*, Paul Lee Tan, ed. (Rockville, MD: 1979), pp. 1476,1477.

[43]*Winning Life's Toughest Battles*, Dr. Julius Segal (NY: McGraw-Hill Book Co., 1986), pp. 46-48.

[44]*Women Who Made a Difference*, Malcolm Forbes (NY: Simon and Schuster, 1990), pp. 245-247.

[45]*Reader's Digest*, April, 1995, pp. 74,75.

[46]*Reader's Digest*, May, 1996, p. 158.

[47]*A 2nd Helping of Chicken Soup for the Soul*, Jack Canfield and Mark Victor Hansen (Deerfield Beach, FL: Health Communications, 1995), pp. 283-287.

[48]*They Rose Above It*, Bob Consodine (Garden City, NY: Doubleday & Co., 1977), p. 108.

[49]*The Road to Faith*, Will Oursler (NY: Rinehart & Co., 1960), pp. 104-106.

[50]*Reader's Digest*, April, 1995, p. 25.

[51]*Illustrations Unlimited*, James Hewett, ed. (Wheaton, IL: Tyndale House, 1988), p. 471.

[52]*The New Dynamics of Winning*, Denis Waitley (NY: William Morrow & Co., 1993), pp. 122-124.

[53]*A 3rd Serving of Chicken Soup for the Soul*, Jack Canfield and Mark Victor Hansen (Deerfield Beach, FL: Health Communications, 1996), pp. 299-302.

[54]*Knight's Treasury of 2,000 Illustrations*, Walter B. Knight (Grand Rapids, MI: Wm. B. Eerdman's Publishing Co., 1963), p. 325.

[55]*San Luis Obispo County Telegram-Tribune*, August 30, 1996, p. B1.

[56]*It's Always Too Soon to Quit*, Lewis R. Timberlake (Grand Rapids, MI: Fleming H. Revell, 1988), pp. 20,21.

[57]*Illustrations Unlimited*, James Hewett, ed. (Wheaton, IL: Tyndale House, 1988), pp. 168,169.

[58]*Success Is Never Ending*, Failure Is Never Final, Robert H. Schuller (Nashville, TN: Thomas Nelson Publishers, 1989), pp. 64,65.

[59]*Reader's Digest*, November, 1994, pp. 226-247.

[60]*Encyclopedia of Sermon Illustrations*, David F. Burgess (St. Louis, MO: Concordia Publishing House, 1964), p. 41.

[61]*Your Money or Your Life*, Joe Dominguez and Vicki Robin (NY: Penguin Books, 1992), pp. 255,256.

[62]*Living More with Less*, Doris Jansen Longacre (Scottsdale, PA: Herald Press, 1980), p. 179.

[63]*Illustrations for Preaching and Teaching*, Craig Brian Larson, ed. (Grand Rapids, MI: Baker Books, 1993), p. 222.

[64]*Earl Nightingale's Greatest Discovery*, Earl Nightingale (NY: Dodd, Mead & Co., 1987), pp. 102,103.

[65]*Reader's Digest*, March, 1996, pp. 63-65.

[66]*Encyclopedia of 7700 Illustrations*, Paul Lee Tan ed. (Rockville, MD: Assurance Publishers, 1979), p. 619.

[67]*Reader's Digest*, October, 1996, pp. 94-99.

[68]*Reader's Digest*, October, 1996, pp. 52-57, 193-228.

[69]*Bible Power for Successful Living*, Norman Vincent Peale (Grand Rapids, MI: Fleming H. Revell, 1993), pp. 64,65.

[70]*Taking Chances*, Dr. Robert T. Lewis (Boston: Houghton Mifflin Co., 1979), pp. 135,136.

[71]*Illustrations Unlimited*, James S. Hewett, ed. (Wheaton, IL: Tyndale, 1988), pp. 270,271.

[72]*Illustrations Unlimited*, James Hewett, ed. (Wheaton, IL: Tyndale House, 1988), pp. 470,471.

[73]*Reader's Digest*, August, 1995, pp. 107,108.

[74]*It's Always Too Soon to Quit*, Lewis R. Timberlake (Grand Rapids, MI: Fleming H. Revell, 1988), p. 21.

[75]*Illustrations Unlimited*, James S. Hewett, ed. (Wheaton, IL: Tyndale, 1988), p. 185.

[76]*One Door Closes, Another Door Opens*, Arthur Pine (NY: Dell Trade Paperback, 1993), pp. 60,61.

[77]*Illustrations Unlimited*, James S. Hewett, ed. (Wheaton, IL: Tyndale House, 1988), p. 185.

[78]*The Best-Loved Poems of the American People*, Hazel Felleman, ed. (NY: Doubleday, 1936) pp. 88,89.

[79]*Reader's Digest*, June, 1996, p. 113,114.

[80]*Encyclopedia of 7700 Illustrations*, Paul Lee Tan (Rockville, MD: Assurance Publishers, 1979), p. 1001.

[81]*Reader's Digest*, March, 1996, pp. 43,44.

[82]*Reader's Digest*, November, 1995, pp. 129-132.

[83]*Encyclopedia of Sermon Illustrations*, David F. Burgess (St. Louis, MO: Concordia Publishing House, 1984), p. 47.

[84]*San Luis Obispo County Telegram-Tribune*, August 23, 1996, A2.

[85]*Science*, August, 1996, pp. 1043-1045.

[86]*Reader's Digest*, June, 1996, pp. 109,110.

[87]*Knight's Treasury of 2,000 Illustrations*, Walter B. Knight (Grand Rapids, MI: Wm. B. Eerdmans Publishing Co., 1963), p. 358.

[88]*The New Dynamics of Winning*, Denis Waitley (NY: Wm. Morrow & Co., Inc., 1993), pp. 17-20.

[89]*Reader's Digest*, March 1995, pp. 178-180.

[90]*Illustrations for Preaching and Teaching*, Craig Brian Larson (Grand Rapids, MI: Baker Books, 1993), p. 7.

[91]*Loving God*, Charles Colson (Grand Rapids, MI: Zondervan Publishing House, 1983, 1987), pp. 132,133.

[92]*The Achievement Factors*, B. Eugene Griessman (NY: Dodd, Mead & Co., 1987), pp. 29,30.

[93]*Women Who Made a Difference*, Malcolm Forbes (NY: Simon and Schuster, 1990), pp. 82-84.

[94]*When Smart People Fail*, Carole Hyatt and Linda Gottleib (NY: Simon and Schuster, 1987), pp. 21-23.

[95]*Reader's Digest*, March, 1996, p. 107.

[96]*Knight's Master Book of 4,000 Illustrations,* Walter B. Knight, (Grand Rapids, MI: Wm. B. Eerdmans Publishing Co., 1956), p. 175.

[97]*The Body*, Charles Colson with Ellen Santilli Vaugh (Dallas, TX: Word Publishing, 1992), pp. 105,106.

[98]*Reader's Digest*, May, 1996, pp. 157,158.

[99]*Illustrations Unlimited*, James S. Hewett, ed. (Wheaton, IL: Tyndale House, 1988), pp. 469,470.

[100]*Norman Vincent Peale's Treasury of Courage and Confidence*, Norman Vincent Peale, ed. (Garden City, NY: Doubleday & Co., 1970), pp. 1,2.

[101]*Reader's Digest*, October, 1993, p. 126.

[102]*Women Who Made a Difference*, Malcolm Forbes (NY: Simon and Schuster, 1990), pp. 17,18.

[103]*Loving God*, Charles Colson (Grand Rapids, MI: Zondervan Publishing House, 1983, 1987), pp. 21-25.

[104]*Reader's Digest*, June, 1996, pp. 110,111.

[105]*Bible Power for Successful Living*, Norman Vincent Peale (Grand Rapids, MI: Fleming H. Revell, 1993), pp. 86,87.

[106]*You're Smarter Than You Think*, Seymour Epstein, Ph.D. with Archie Brodsky (NY: Simon and Schuster, 1993), p. 131.

[107]*The Greatest Success in the World*, Og Mandino (Toronto: Bantam Books, 1981), pp. 93,94.

[108]*Illustrations Unlimited,* James S. Hewett, ed. (Wheaton, IL: Tyndale House, 1988), p. 155.

[109]*Best Loved Poems of the American People*, Hazel Felleman, ed. (NY: Doubleday, 1936), p. 89.

[110]*Illustrations Unlimited,* James S. Hewett, ed. (Wheaton, IL: Tyndale, 1988), pp. 468,469.

[111]*Knight's Treasury of 2,000 Illustrations*, Walter B. Knight (Grand Rapids, MI: Wm. B. Eerdmans Publishing Co., 1963), p. 358.

[112]*The Body*, Charles Colson with Ellen Santilli Vaughn (Dallas, TX: Word Publishing, 1992), pp. 301-303.

[113]*It's Always Too Soon to Quit*, Lewis R. Timberlake (Grand Rapids, MI: Fleming H. Revell, 1988), pp. 51,52.

[114]*Knight's Master Book of 4,000 Illustrations*, Walter B. Knight (Grand Rapids, MI: Wm. B. Eerdmans Publishing Co., 1956), p. 127.

[115]*San Luis Obispo County Telegram-Tribune*, August 31, 1996, p. C1.

[116]*A 2nd Helping of Chicken Soup for the Soul*, Jack Canfield and Mark Victor Hansen (Deerfield Beach, FL: Health Communications, 1996), pp. 235,236.

[117]*Knight's Master Book of 4,000 Illustrations*, Walter B. Knight (Grand Rapids, MI: Wm. B. Eerdmans Publishing Co., 1956), p. 473.

[118]*Taking Chances*, Dr. Robert T. Lewis (Boston: Houghton Mifflin, 1979), pp. 190,191.

[119]*The Achievement Factors*, B. Eugene Griessman (NY: Dodd, Mead & Co., 1987), pp. 54,55.

[120]*Illustrations for Preaching and Teaching*, Craig Brian Larson (Grand Rapids, MI: Baker Books, 1993), p. 267.

[121]*San Luis Obispo County Telegram-Tribune*, August 31, 1996, p. B1.

[122]*One Door Closes, Another Door Opens*, Arthur Pine (NY: Dell Trade Paperback, 1993), pp. 31,32.

[123]*Knight's Treasury of 2,000 Illustrations*, Walter B. Knight (Grand Rapids, MI: Wm. B. Eerdmans Publishing Co., 1963), p. 300.

[124]*First Things First*, Stephen R. Covey, A. Roger Merrill, Rebecca R. Merrill (NY: Simon and Schuster, 1994), pp. 68,69.

[125]*Reader's Digest*, May, 1994, p. 114.

[126]*Illustrations Unlimited*, James S. Hewett, ed. (Wheaton, IL: Tyndale House, 1988), p. 475.

[127]*Glorious Intruder*, Joni Eareckson Tada (Portland, OR: Multnomah, 1989), p. 148.

[128]*It's Always Too Soon to Quit*, Lewis R. Timberlake (Grand Rapids, MI: Fleming H. Revell, 1988), pp. 76,77.

[129]*Illustrations Unlimited*, James S. Hewett, ed. (Wheaton, IL: Tyndale House, 1988), p. 466.

[130]*From Bad Beginnings to Happy Endings*, Ed Young (Nashville, TN: Thomas Nelson, 1994), pp. 27,28.

[131]*Illustrations Unlimited*, James S. Hewett, ed. (Wheaton, IL: Tyndale House, 1988), p. 468.

[132]*Dr. Livingstone, I Presume?*, Ian Anstruther (NY: E. P. Dutton and Co., 1957), pp. 51,52.

[133]*A 2nd Helping of Chicken Soup for the Soul*, Jack Canfield and Mark Victor Hansen (Deerfield Beach, FL: Health Communications, 1995), pp. 288-291.

[134]*Encyclopedia of 7700 Illustrations*, Paul Lee Tan, ed. (Rockville, MD: Assurance Publishers, 1979), p. 616.

[135]*Glorious Intruder*, Joni Eareckson Tada (Portland, OR: Multnomah, 1989), p. 156.

[136]*It's Always Too Soon to Quit*, Lewis R. Timberlake (Grand Rapids, MI: Fleming H. Revell, 1988), pp. 18,19.

[137]*Illustrations for Preaching and Teaching*, Craig Brian Larson (Grand Rapids, MI: Baker Books, 1993), p. 250.

[138]*The Body*, Charles Colson with Ellen Santilli Vaughn (Dallas, TX: Word Publishing, 1992), pp. 48,49.

[139]*Illustrations Unlimited*, James S. Hewett, ed. (Wheaton, IL: Tyndale, 1988), pp. 169,170.

[140]*Illustrations Unlimited*, James Hewett ed. (Wheaton, IL: Tyndale, 1988), p. 491.

[141]*From Bad Beginnings to Happy Endings*, Ed Young (Nashville, TN: Thomas Nelson Publishers, 1994), pp. 154,155.

[142]*One Door Closes, Another Door Opens*, Arthur Pine (NY: Dell Trade Paperback, 1993), pp. 13,14.

[143]*Illustrations Unlimited*, James S. Hewett, ed. (Wheaton, IL: Tyndale, 1988), p. 290.

[144]*Illustrations for Preaching and Teaching*, Craig Brian Larson (Grand Rapids, MI: Baker Books, 1993), p. 12.

[145]*It's Always Too Soon to Quit*, Lewis R. Timberlake (Grand Rapids, MI: Fleming H. Revell, 1988), pp. 150-152.

[146]*The Book of Virtues*, William J. Bennett, ed. (NY: Simon and Schuster, 1993), pp. 305,306.

[147]*Loving God*, Charles Colson (Grand Rapids, MI: Zondervan Publishing House, 1983, 1987), pp. 138,139.

Additional copies of this book and other titles in the *God's Little Instruction Book* series are available at your local bookstore.

*God's Little Instruction Book*
*God's Little Instruction Book II*
*God's Little Instruction Book III*
*God's Little Instruction Book on Love*
*God's Little Instruction Book on Prayer*
*God's Little Instruction Book on Success*
*God's Little Instruction Book on Character*
*God's Little Instruction Book for New Believers*
*God's Little Instruction Book for Women —Special Gift Edition*
*God's Little Instruction Book for Men —Special Gift Edition*

HB
HONOR
BOOKS

**Honor Books**
Tulsa, Oklahoma